WOODY & THE NOBLE

Created by
Jason Pell

Pencilled and inked
by Juan Romera

ARCANA
www.arcana.com

CEO and Owner	VP of Operations	Exec. Administrator
Sean O'Reilly	**Mark Poulton**	**Emma Waddell**
VP of Special Projects	Senior Editor	General Manager
Nick Schley	**Mike Kalvoda**	**Michelle Meyers**

Chapter 1

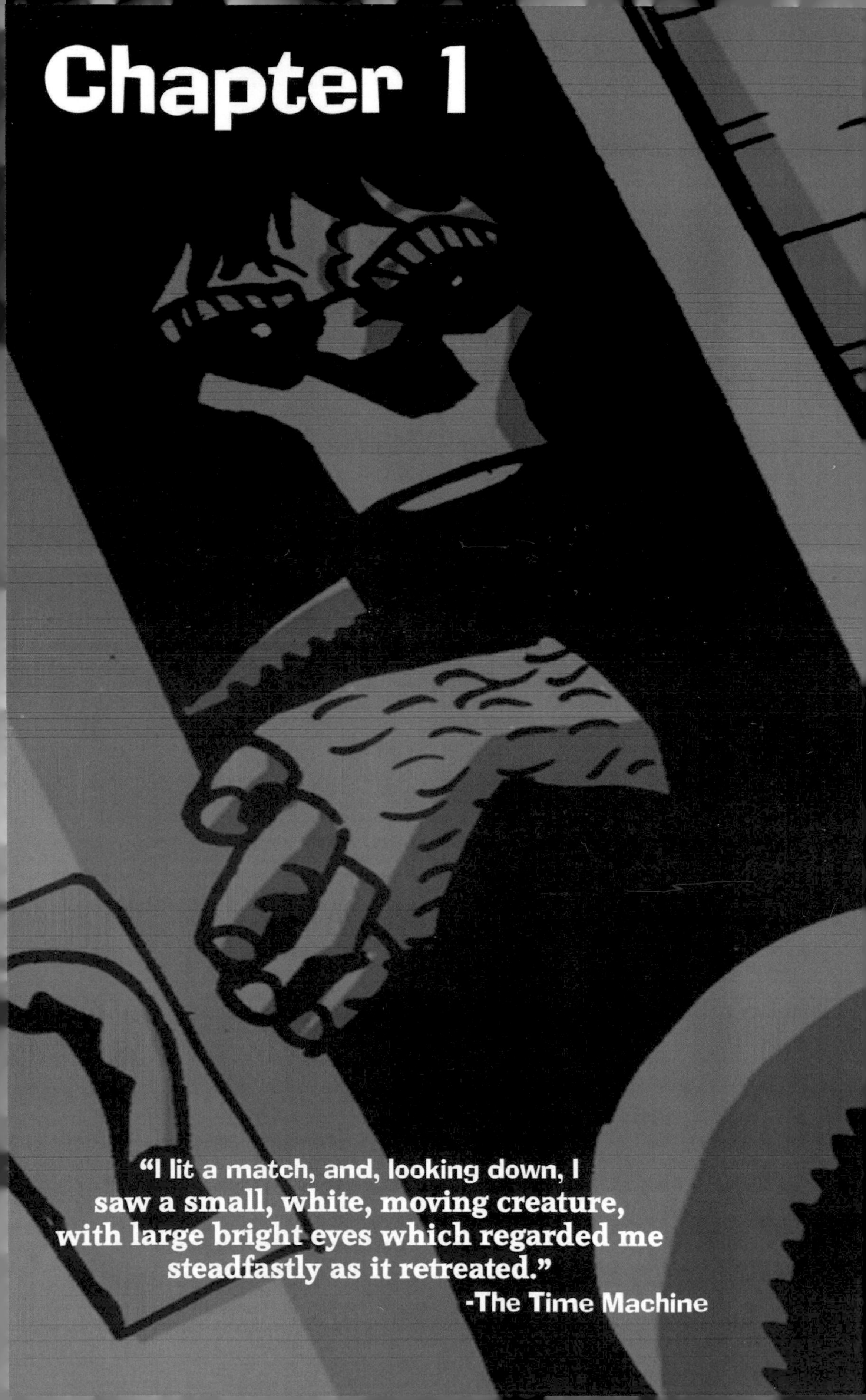

"I lit a match, and, looking down, I saw a small, white, moving creature, with large bright eyes which regarded me steadfastly as it retreated."

-The Time Machine

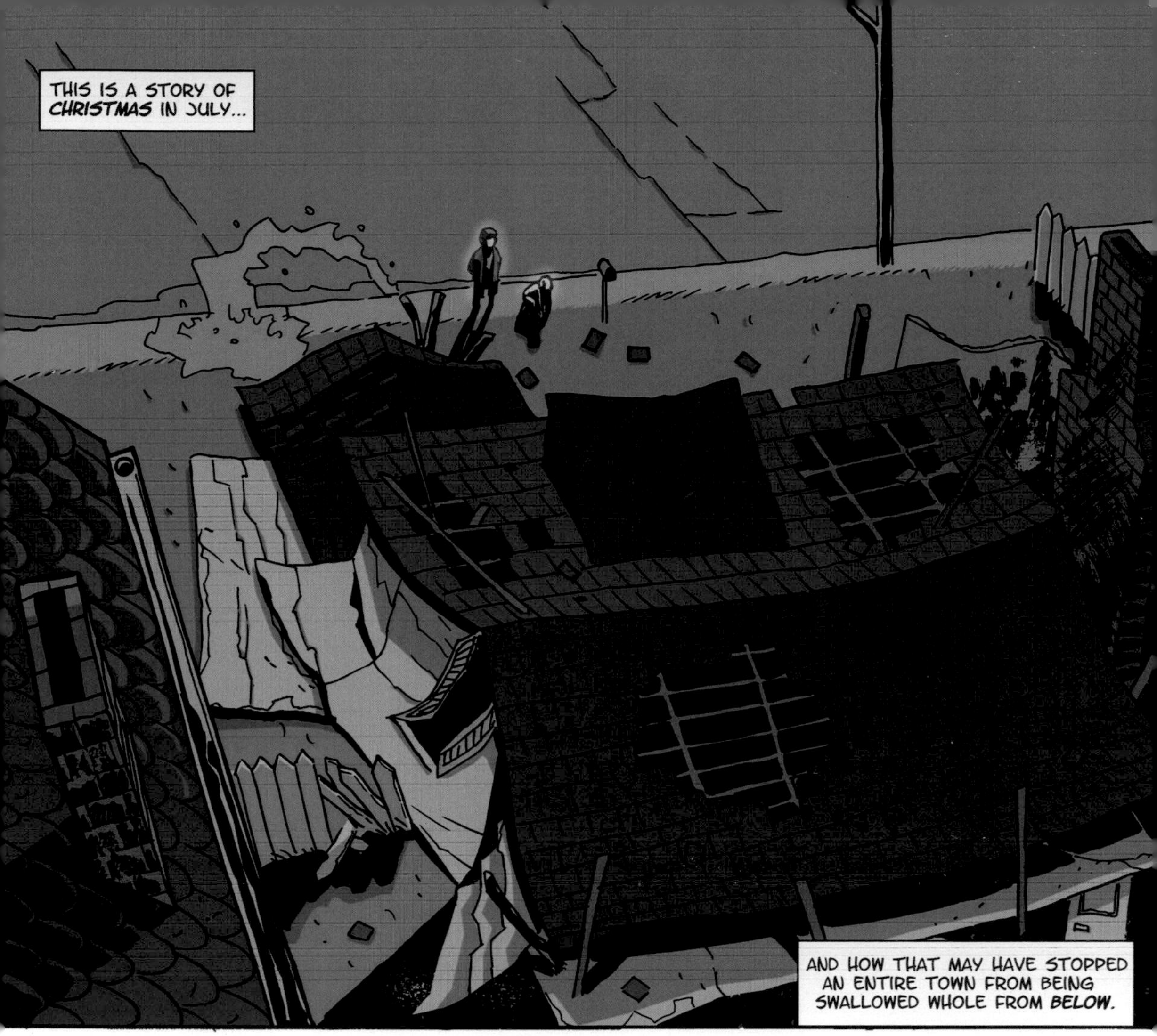
THIS IS A STORY OF CHRISTMAS IN JULY...
AND HOW THAT MAY HAVE STOPPED AN ENTIRE TOWN FROM BEING SWALLOWED WHOLE FROM BELOW.

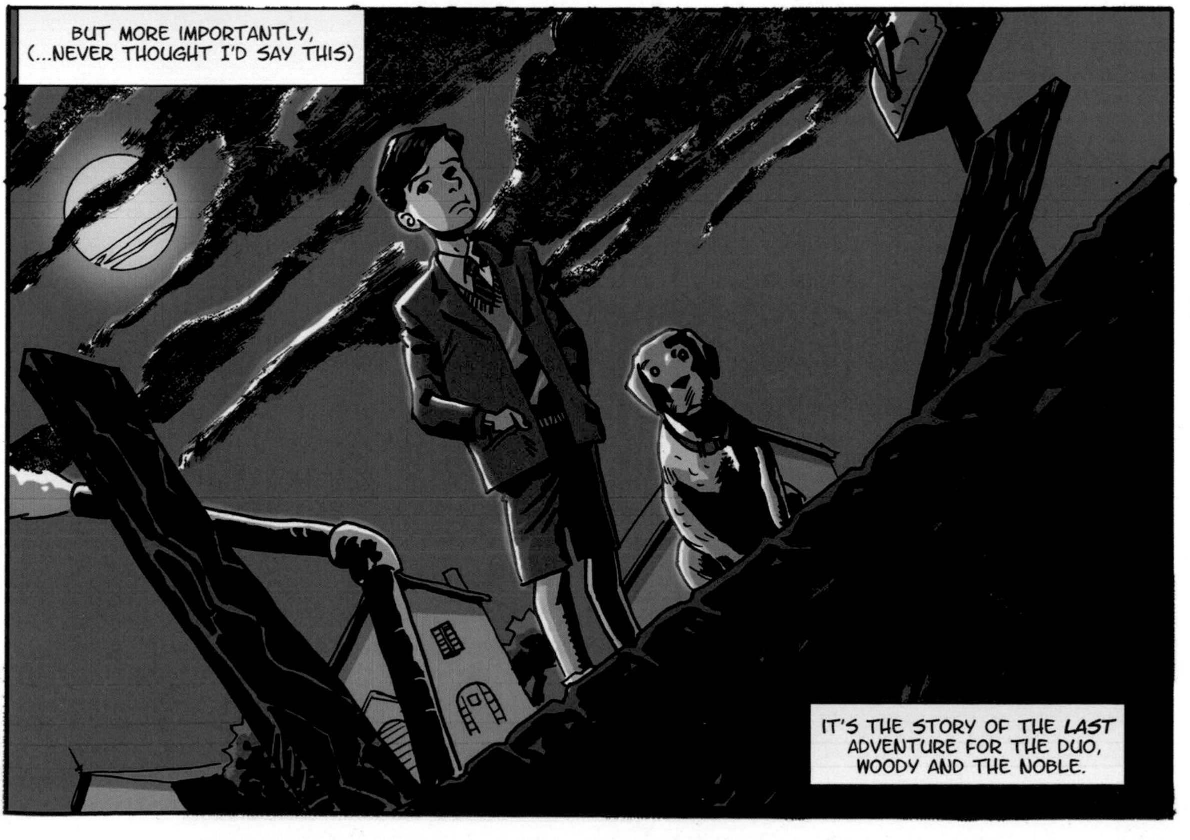
BUT MORE IMPORTANTLY, (...NEVER THOUGHT I'D SAY THIS)
IT'S THE STORY OF THE LAST ADVENTURE FOR THE DUO, WOODY AND THE NOBLE.

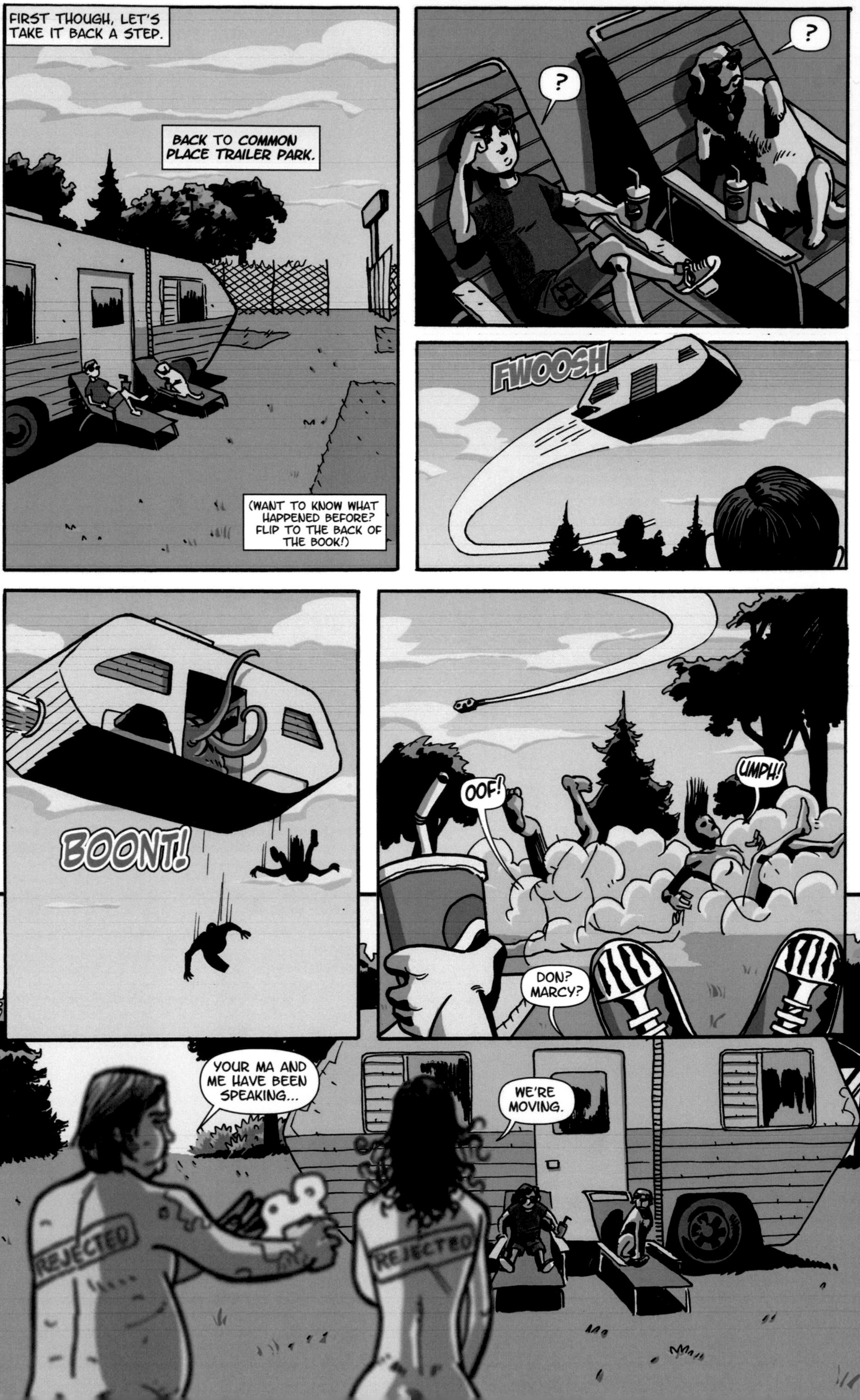
FIRST THOUGH, LET'S TAKE IT BACK A STEP.
BACK TO COMMON PLACE TRAILER PARK.
(WANT TO KNOW WHAT HAPPENED BEFORE? FLIP TO THE BACK OF THE BOOK!)
?
?
FWOOSH
BOONT!
OOF!
UMPH!
DON? MARCY?
YOUR MA AND ME HAVE BEEN SPEAKING...
WE'RE MOVING.
REJECTED
REJECTED

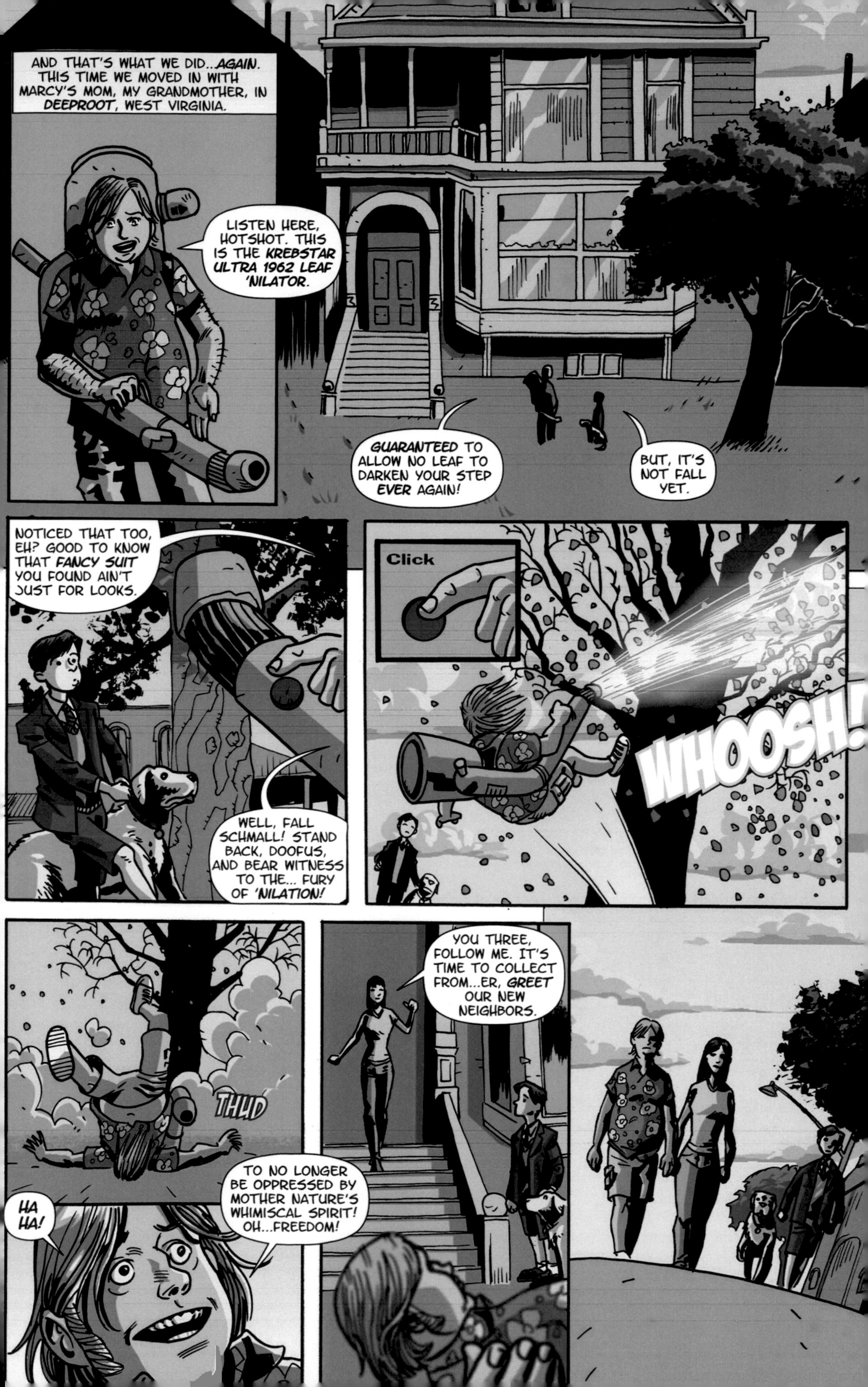
AND THAT'S WHAT WE DID...AGAIN. THIS TIME WE MOVED IN WITH MARCY'S MOM, MY GRANDMOTHER, IN DEEPROOT, WEST VIRGINIA.
LISTEN HERE, HOTSHOT. THIS IS THE KREBSTAR ULTRA 1962 LEAF 'NILATOR.
GUARANTEED TO ALLOW NO LEAF TO DARKEN YOUR STEP EVER AGAIN!
BUT, IT'S NOT FALL YET.
NOTICED THAT TOO, EH? GOOD TO KNOW THAT FANCY SUIT YOU FOUND AIN'T JUST FOR LOOKS.
WELL, FALL SCHMALL! STAND BACK, DOOFUS, AND BEAR WITNESS TO THE... FURY OF 'NILATION!
Click
WHOOSH!
THUD
HA HA!
TO NO LONGER BE OPPRESSED BY MOTHER NATURE'S WHIMSICAL SPIRIT! OH...FREEDOM!
YOU THREE, FOLLOW ME. IT'S TIME TO COLLECT FROM...ER, GREET OUR NEW NEIGHBORS.

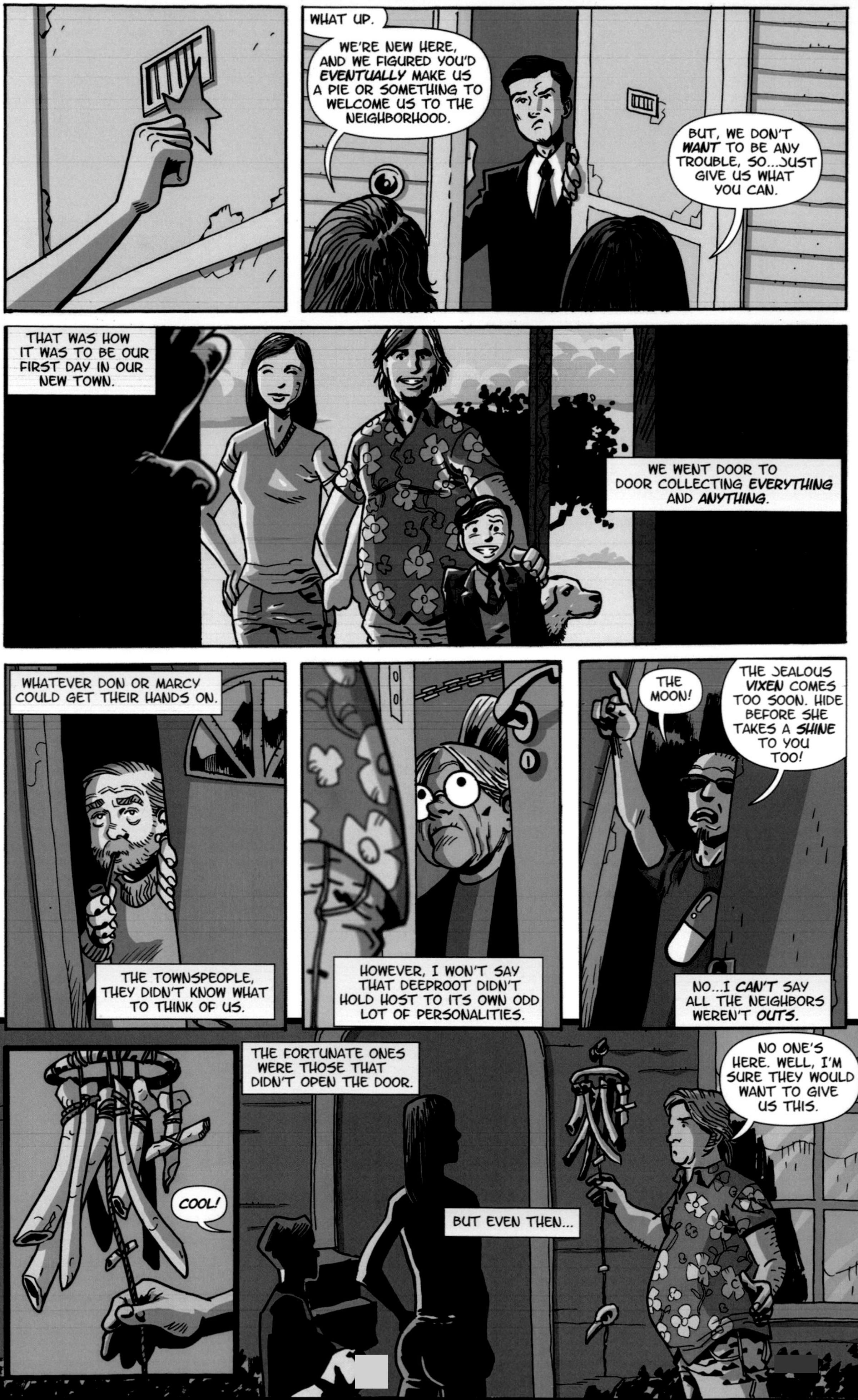
WHAT UP.
WE'RE NEW HERE, AND WE FIGURED YOU'D EVENTUALLY MAKE US A PIE OR SOMETHING TO WELCOME US TO THE NEIGHBORHOOD.
BUT, WE DON'T WANT TO BE ANY TROUBLE, SO...JUST GIVE US WHAT YOU CAN.
THAT WAS HOW IT WAS TO BE OUR FIRST DAY IN OUR NEW TOWN.
WE WENT DOOR TO DOOR COLLECTING EVERYTHING AND ANYTHING.
WHATEVER DON OR MARCY COULD GET THEIR HANDS ON.
THE TOWNSPEOPLE, THEY DIDN'T KNOW WHAT TO THINK OF US.
HOWEVER, I WON'T SAY THAT DEEPROOT DIDN'T HOLD HOST TO ITS OWN ODD LOT OF PERSONALITIES.
THE MOON!
THE JEALOUS VIXEN COMES TOO SOON. HIDE BEFORE SHE TAKES A SHINE TO YOU TOO!
NO...I CAN'T SAY ALL THE NEIGHBORS WEREN'T OUTS.
THE FORTUNATE ONES WERE THOSE THAT DIDN'T OPEN THE DOOR.
COOL!
BUT EVEN THEN...
NO ONE'S HERE. WELL, I'M SURE THEY WOULD WANT TO GIVE US THIS.

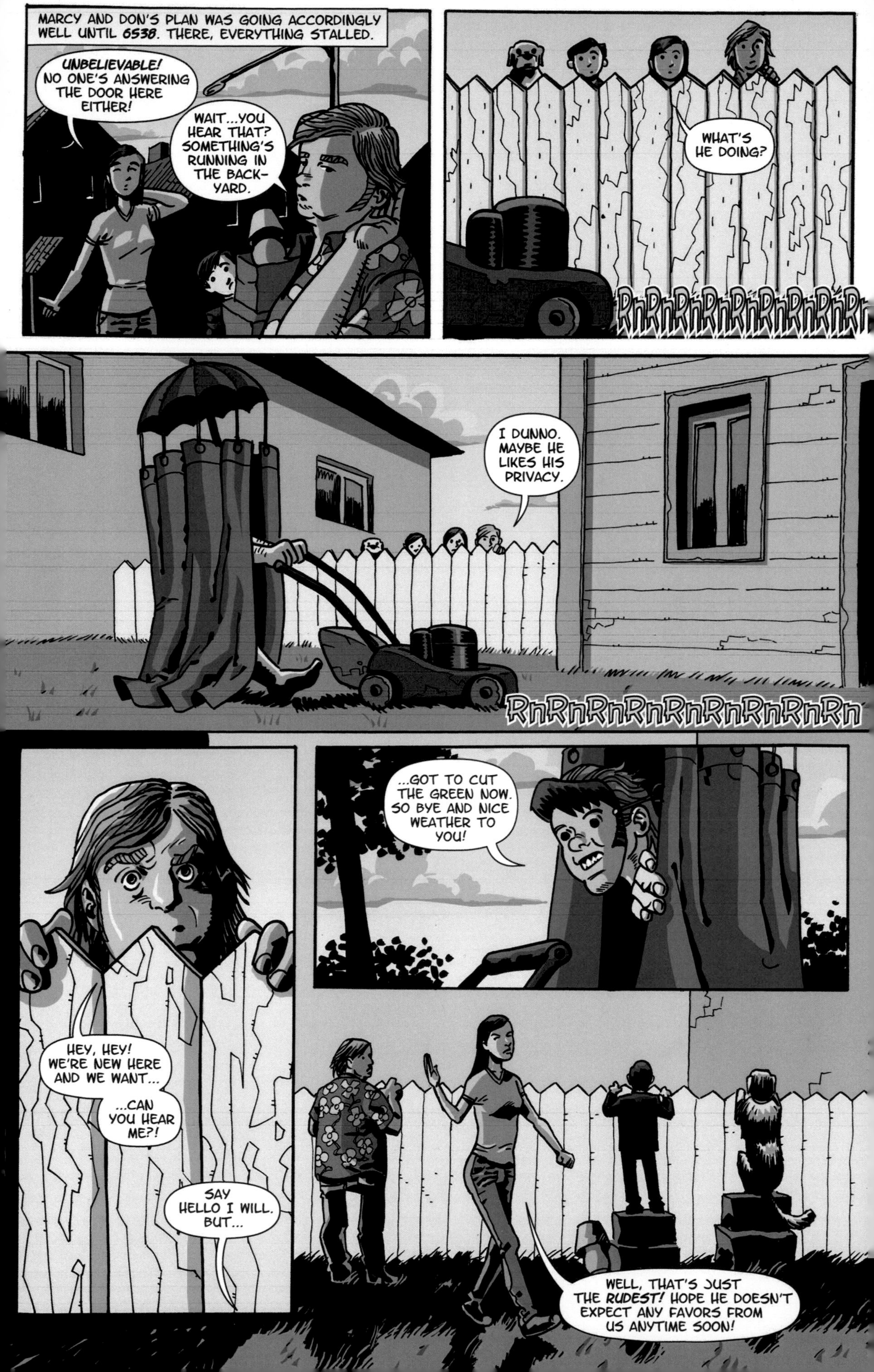
MARCY AND DON'S PLAN WAS GOING ACCORDINGLY WELL UNTIL 6538. THERE, EVERYTHING STALLED.
UNBELIEVABLE! NO ONE'S ANSWERING THE DOOR HERE EITHER!
WAIT...YOU HEAR THAT? SOMETHING'S RUNNING IN THE BACK-YARD.
WHAT'S HE DOING?
RnRnRnRnRnRnRnRnRnRn
I DUNNO. MAYBE HE LIKES HIS PRIVACY.
RnRnRnRnRnRnRnRnRn
HEY, HEY! WE'RE NEW HERE AND WE WANT...
...CAN YOU HEAR ME?!
SAY HELLO I WILL. BUT...
...GOT TO CUT THE GREEN NOW. SO BYE AND NICE WEATHER TO YOU!
WELL, THAT'S JUST THE RUDEST! HOPE HE DOESN'T EXPECT ANY FAVORS FROM US ANYTIME SOON!

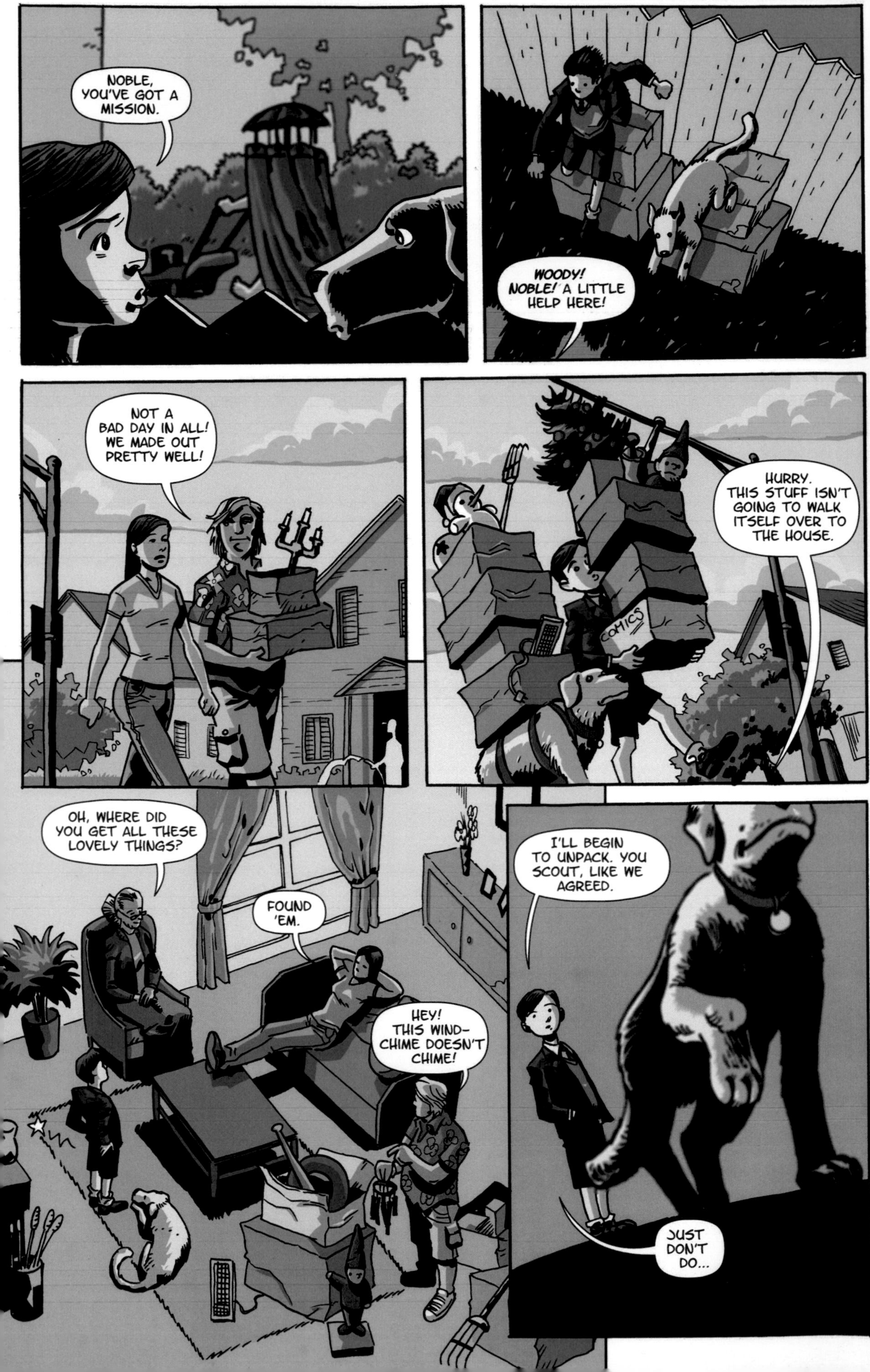
NOBLE, YOU'VE GOT A MISSION.
WOODY! NOBLE! A LITTLE HELP HERE!
NOT A BAD DAY IN ALL! WE MADE OUT PRETTY WELL!
HURRY. THIS STUFF ISN'T GOING TO WALK ITSELF OVER TO THE HOUSE.
COMICS
OH, WHERE DID YOU GET ALL THESE LOVELY THINGS?
FOUND 'EM.
HEY! THIS WIND-CHIME DOESN'T CHIME!
I'LL BEGIN TO UNPACK. YOU SCOUT, LIKE WE AGREED.
JUST DON'T DO...

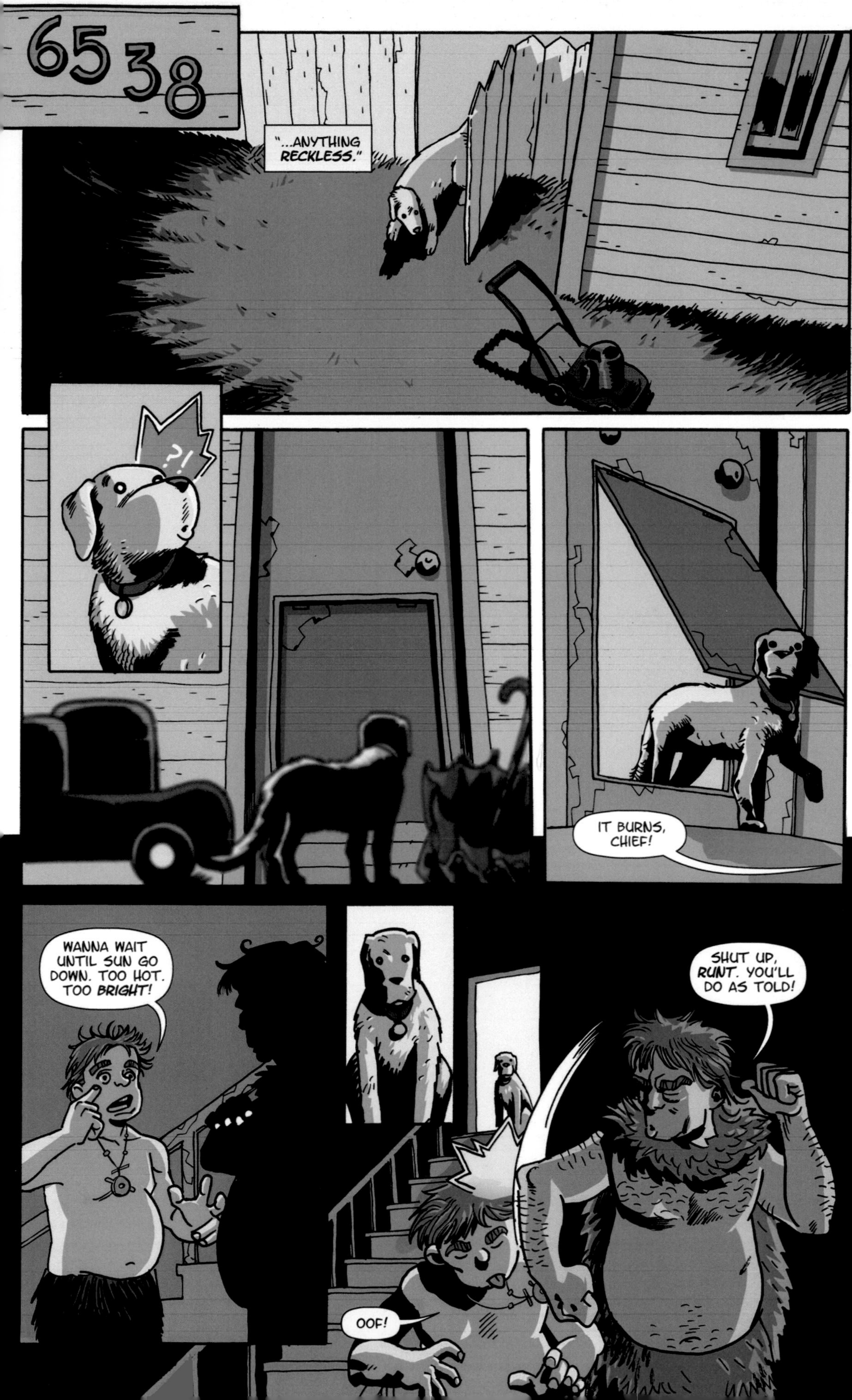
65 38
"...ANYTHING RECKLESS."
?!
IT BURNS, CHIEF!
WANNA WAIT UNTIL SUN GO DOWN. TOO HOT. TOO BRIGHT!
SHUT UP, RUNT. YOU'LL DO AS TOLD!
OOF!

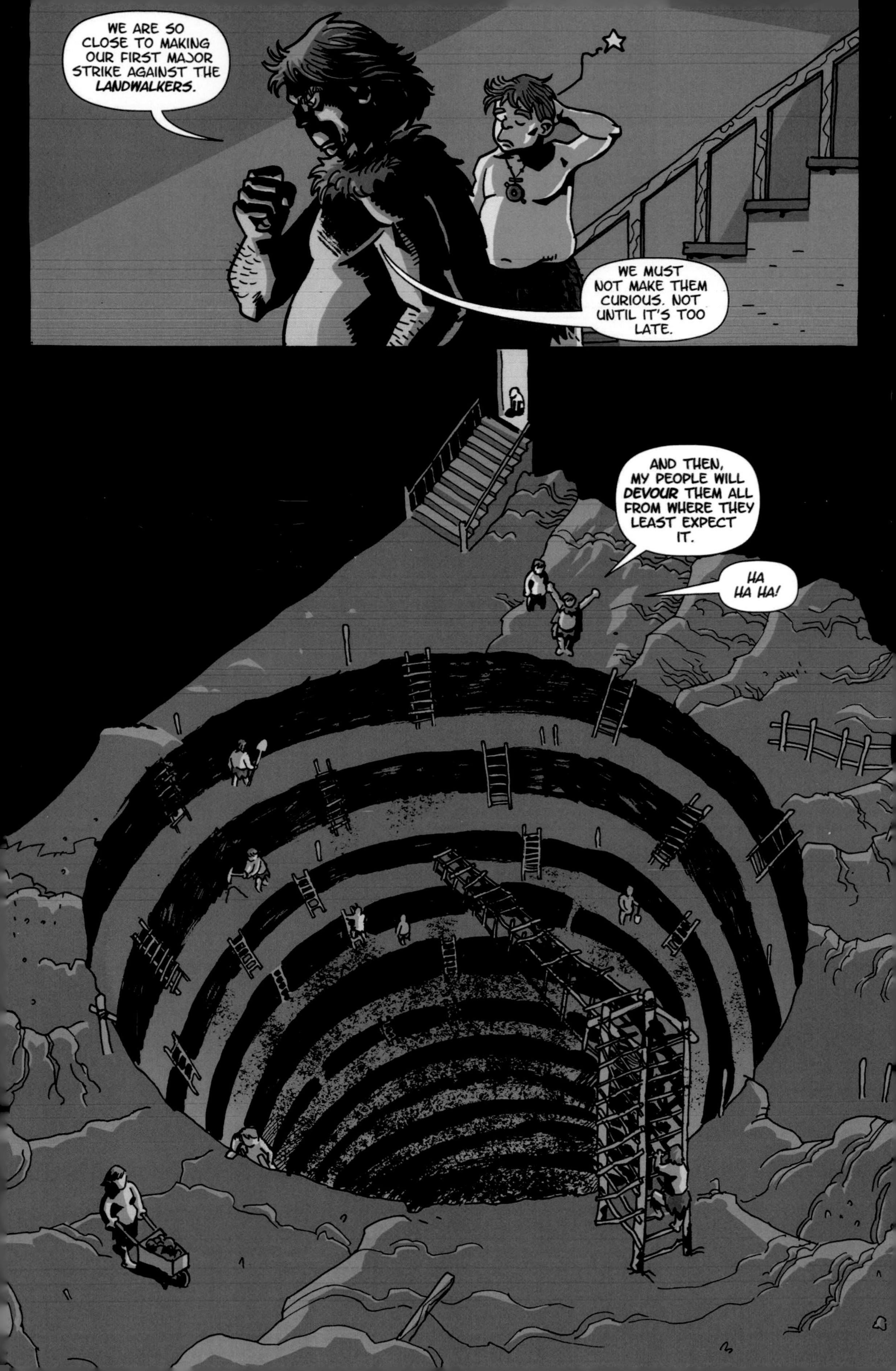
WE ARE SO CLOSE TO MAKING OUR FIRST MAJOR STRIKE AGAINST THE *LANDWALKERS*.
WE MUST NOT MAKE THEM CURIOUS. NOT UNTIL IT'S TOO LATE.
AND THEN, MY PEOPLE WILL **DEVOUR** THEM ALL FROM WHERE THEY LEAST EXPECT IT.
HA HA HA!

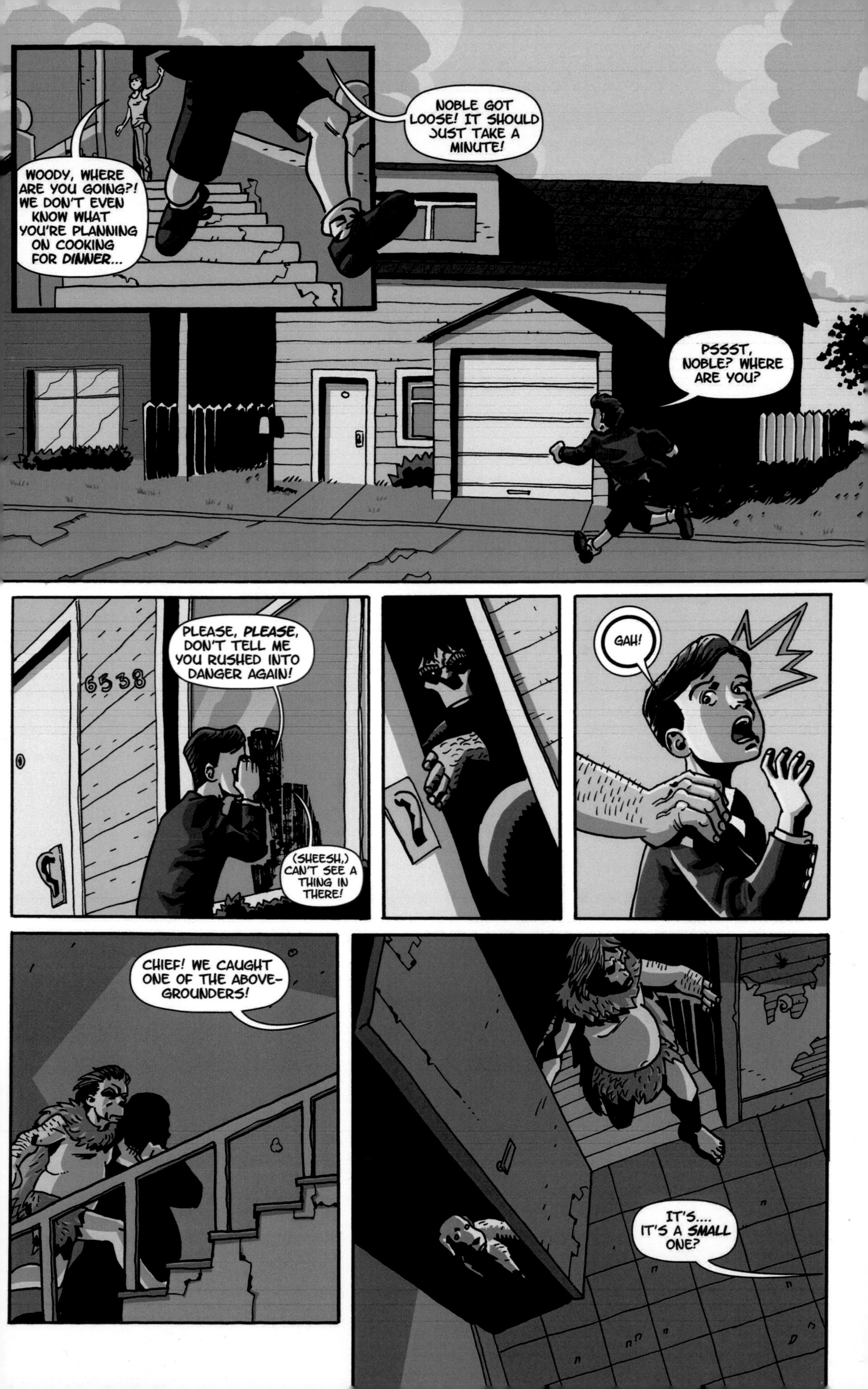
WOODY, WHERE ARE YOU GOING?! WE DON'T EVEN KNOW WHAT YOU'RE PLANNING ON COOKING FOR DINNER...
NOBLE GOT LOOSE! IT SHOULD JUST TAKE A MINUTE!
PSSST, NOBLE? WHERE ARE YOU?
6538
PLEASE, PLEASE, DON'T TELL ME YOU RUSHED INTO DANGER AGAIN!
(SHEESH,) CAN'T SEE A THING IN THERE!
GAH!
CHIEF! WE CAUGHT ONE OF THE ABOVE-GROUNDERS!
IT'S.... IT'S A SMALL ONE?

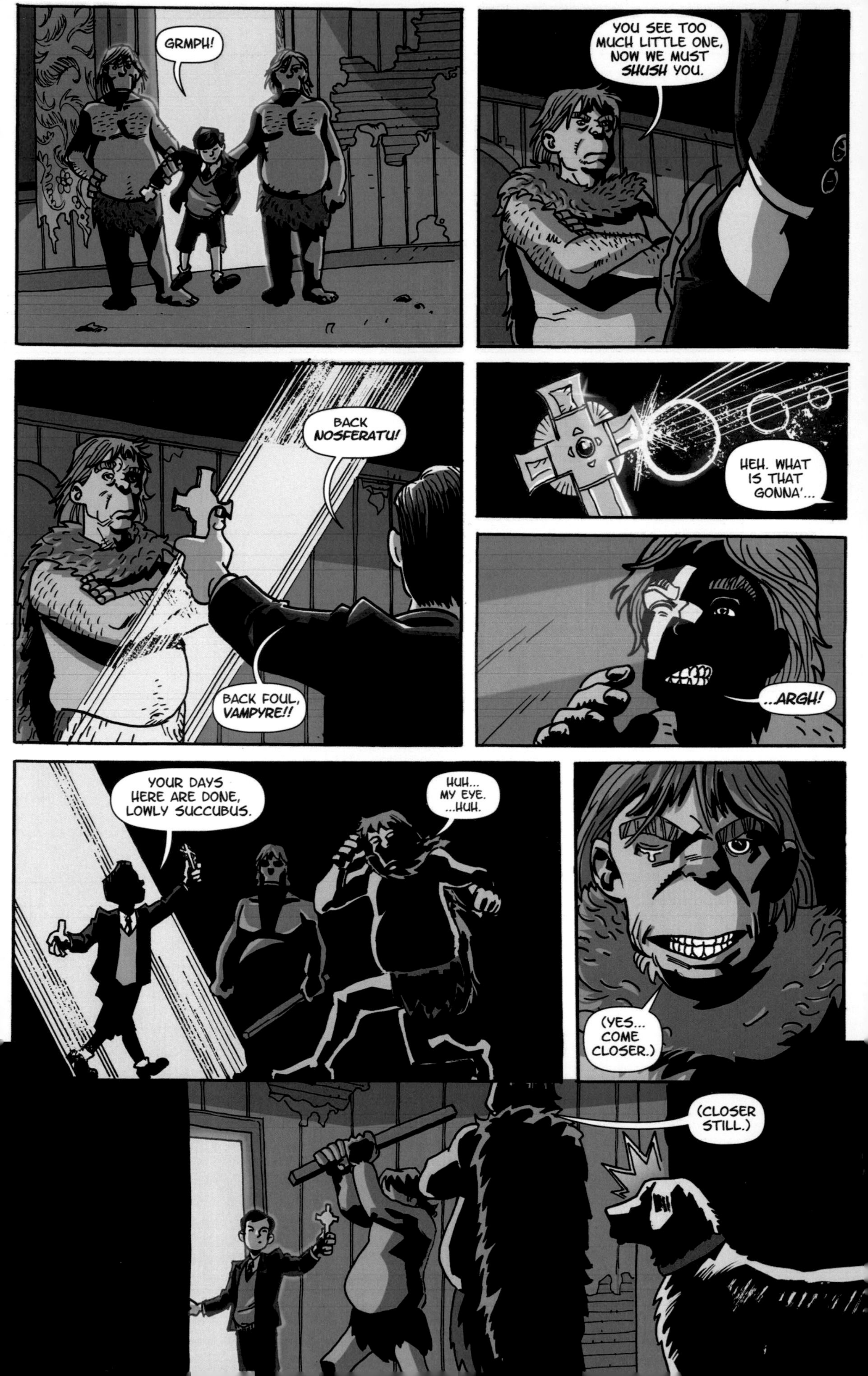
GRMPH!
YOU SEE TOO MUCH LITTLE ONE, NOW WE MUST SHUSH YOU.
BACK NOSFERATU!
BACK FOUL, VAMPYRE!!
HEH. WHAT IS THAT GONNA'...
...ARGH!
YOUR DAYS HERE ARE DONE, LOWLY SUCCUBUS.
HUH... MY EYE. ...HUH.
(YES... COME CLOSER.)
(CLOSER STILL.)

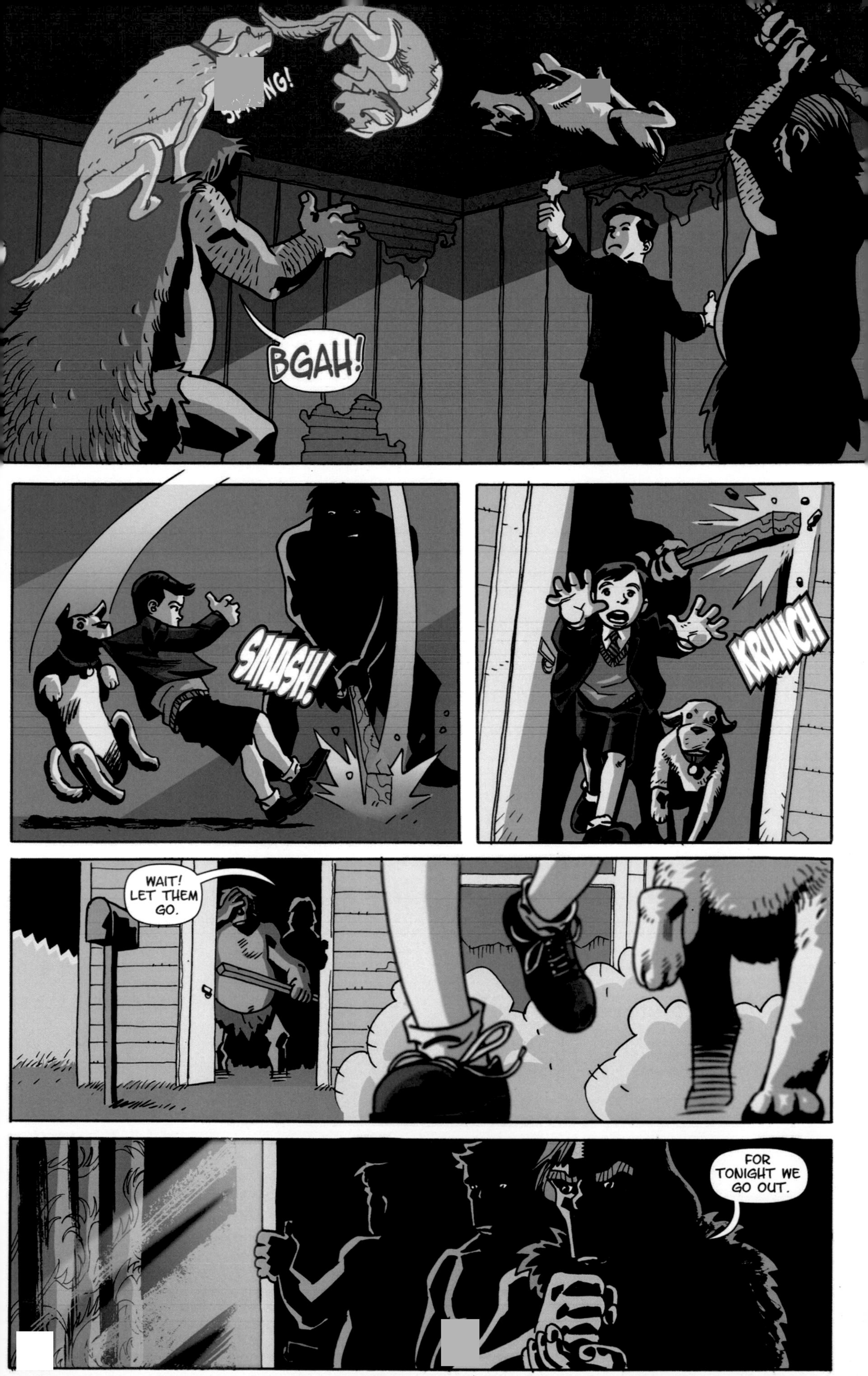
BGAH!
SMASH!
KRUNCH
WAIT! LET THEM GO.
FOR TONIGHT WE GO OUT.

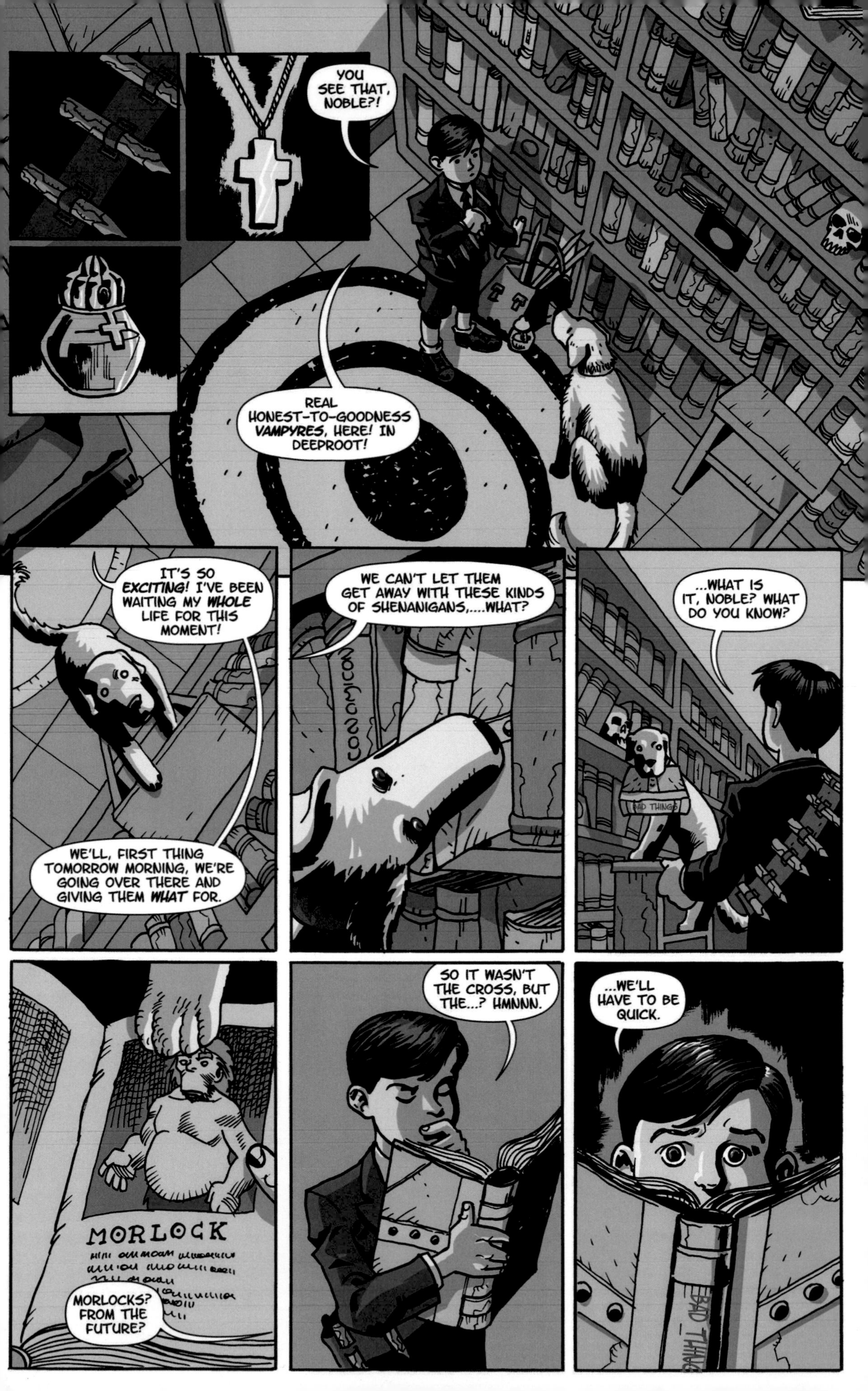
YOU SEE THAT, NOBLE?!
REAL HONEST-TO-GOODNESS VAMPYRES, HERE! IN DEEPROOT!
IT'S SO EXCITING! I'VE BEEN WAITING MY WHOLE LIFE FOR THIS MOMENT!
WE'LL, FIRST THING TOMORROW MORNING, WE'RE GOING OVER THERE AND GIVING THEM WHAT FOR.
WE CAN'T LET THEM GET AWAY WITH THESE KINDS OF SHENANIGANS,....WHAT?
CONOMICON
...WHAT IS IT, NOBLE? WHAT DO YOU KNOW?
BAD THINGS
MORLOCK
MORLOCKS? FROM THE FUTURE?
SO IT WASN'T THE CROSS, BUT THE...? HMNNN.
...WE'LL HAVE TO BE QUICK.

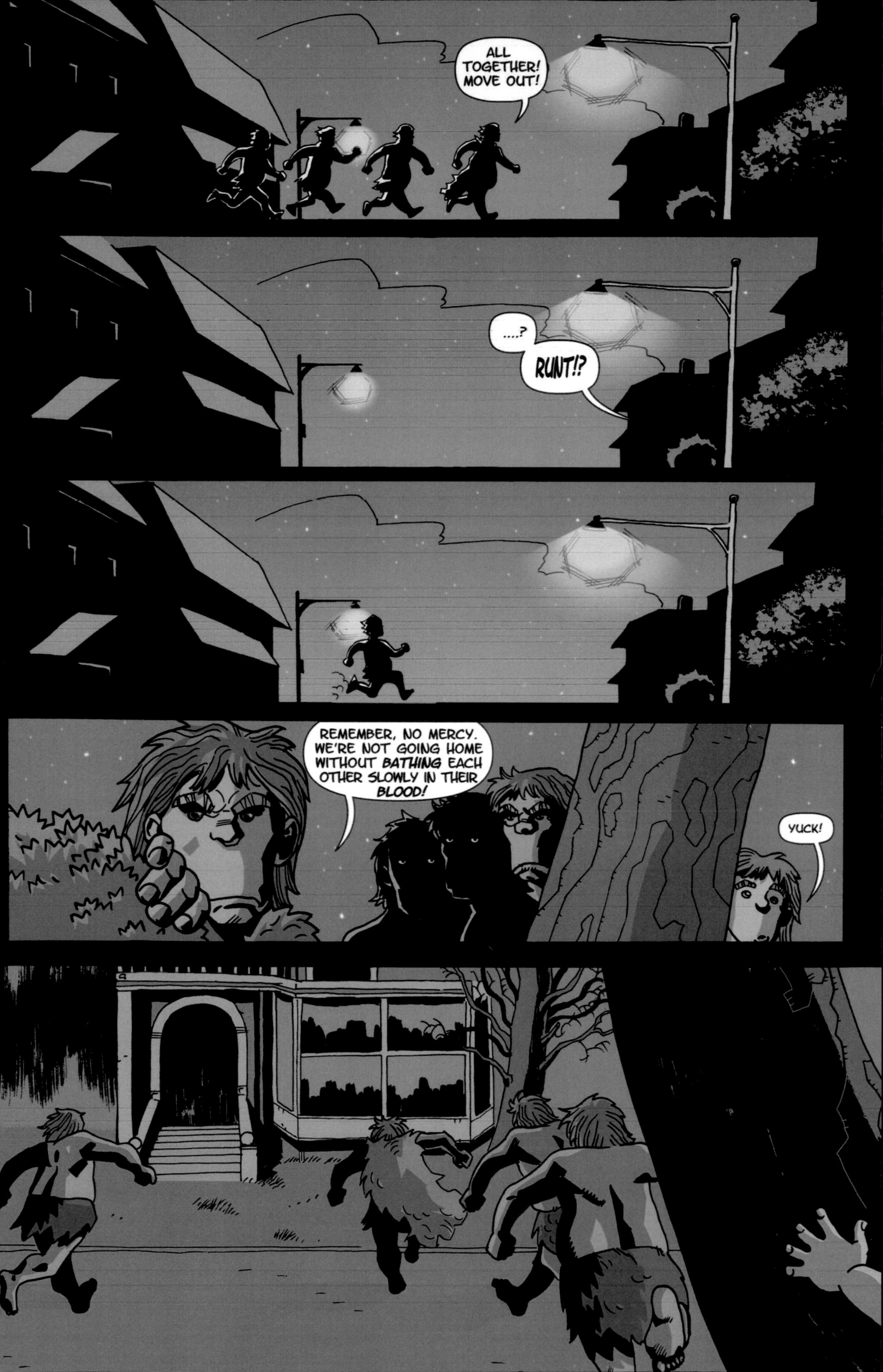
ALL TOGETHER! MOVE OUT!
....?
RUNT!?
REMEMBER, NO MERCY. WE'RE NOT GOING HOME WITHOUT BATHING EACH OTHER SLOWLY IN THEIR BLOOD!
YUCK!

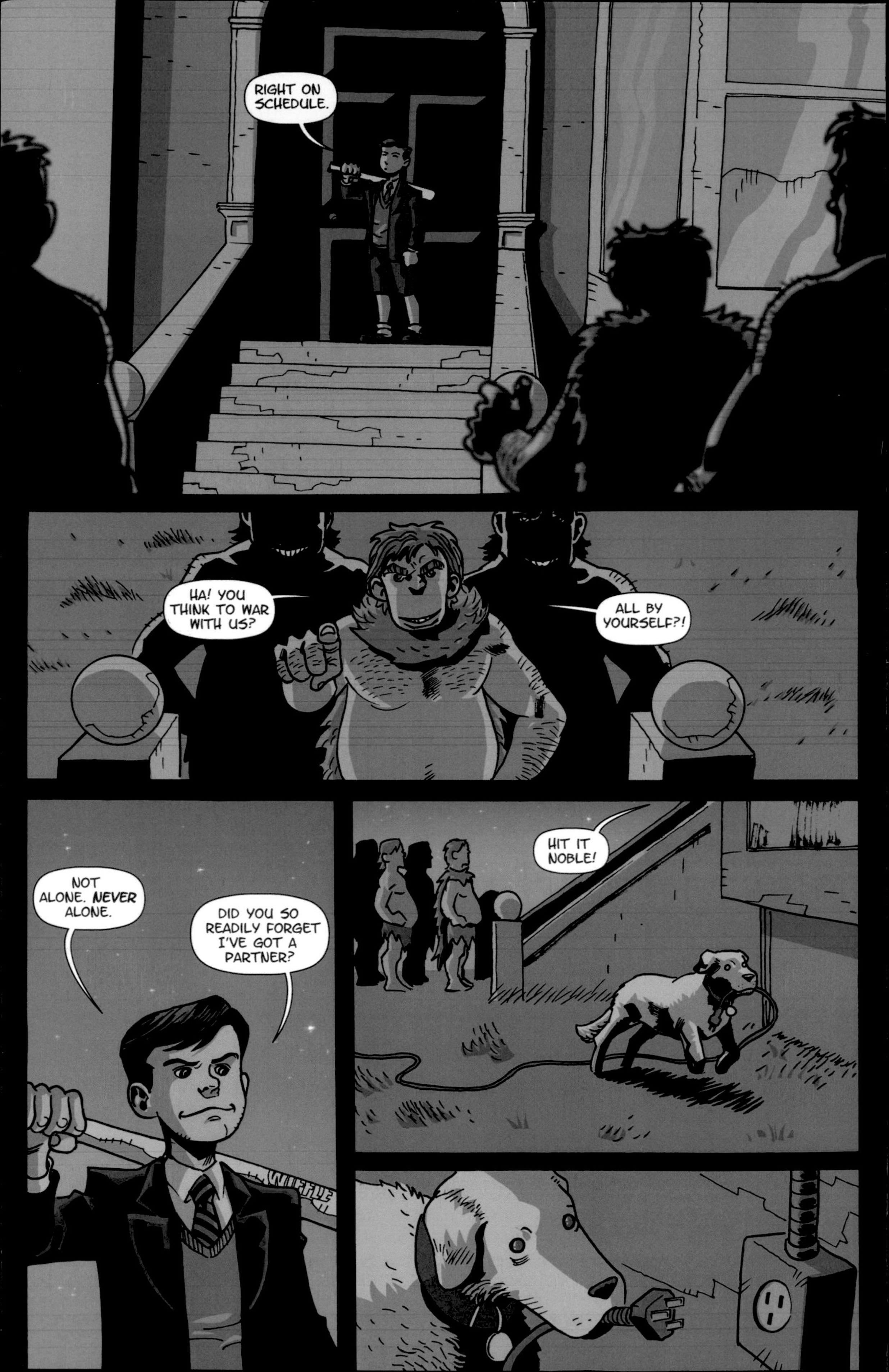
RIGHT ON SCHEDULE.
HA! YOU THINK TO WAR WITH US?
ALL BY YOURSELF?!
NOT ALONE. NEVER ALONE.
DID YOU SO READILY FORGET I'VE GOT A PARTNER?
HIT IT NOBLE!

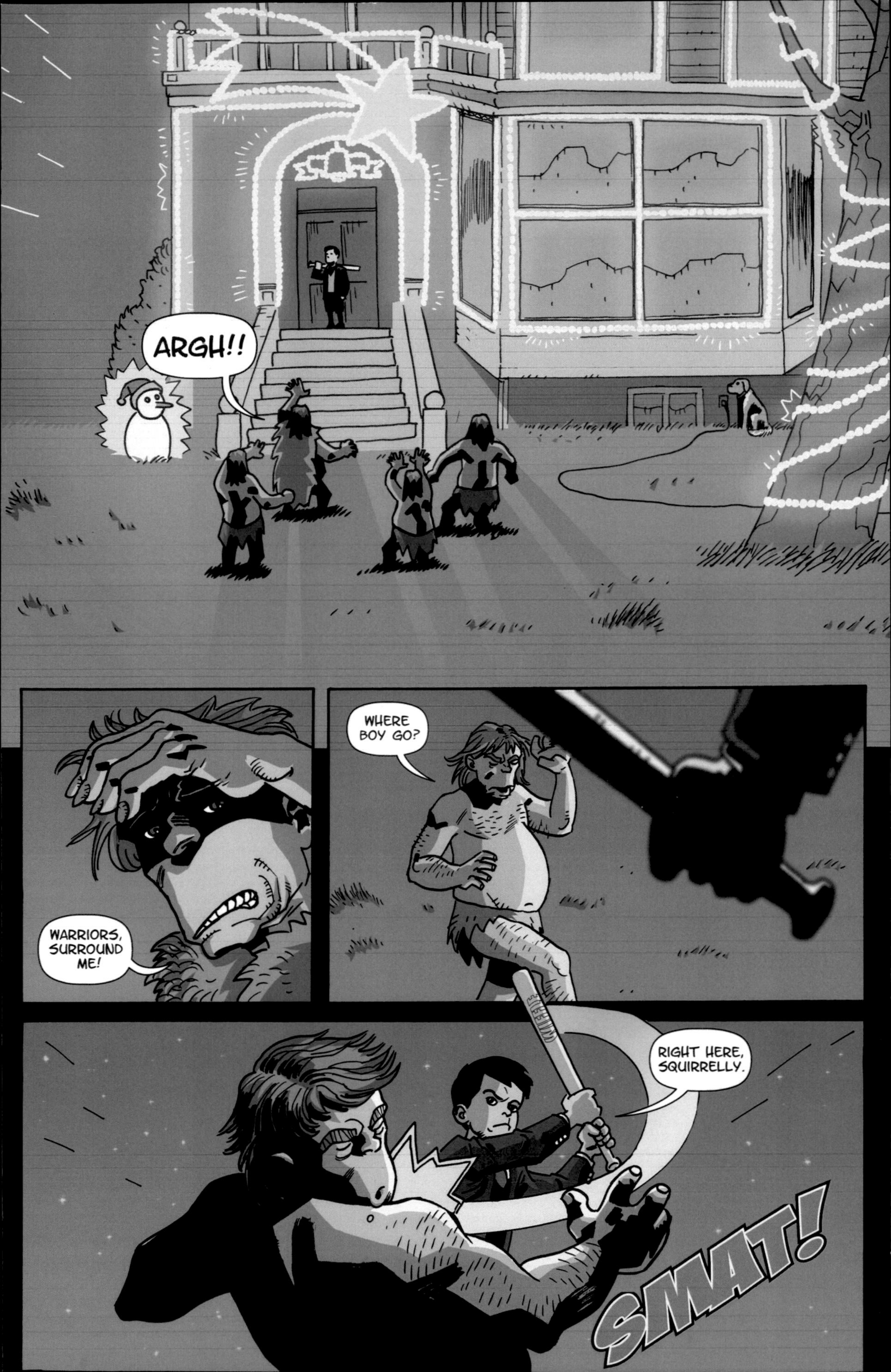
ARGH!!
WARRIORS, SURROUND ME!
WHERE BOY GO?
RIGHT HERE, SQUIRRELLY.
SMAT!

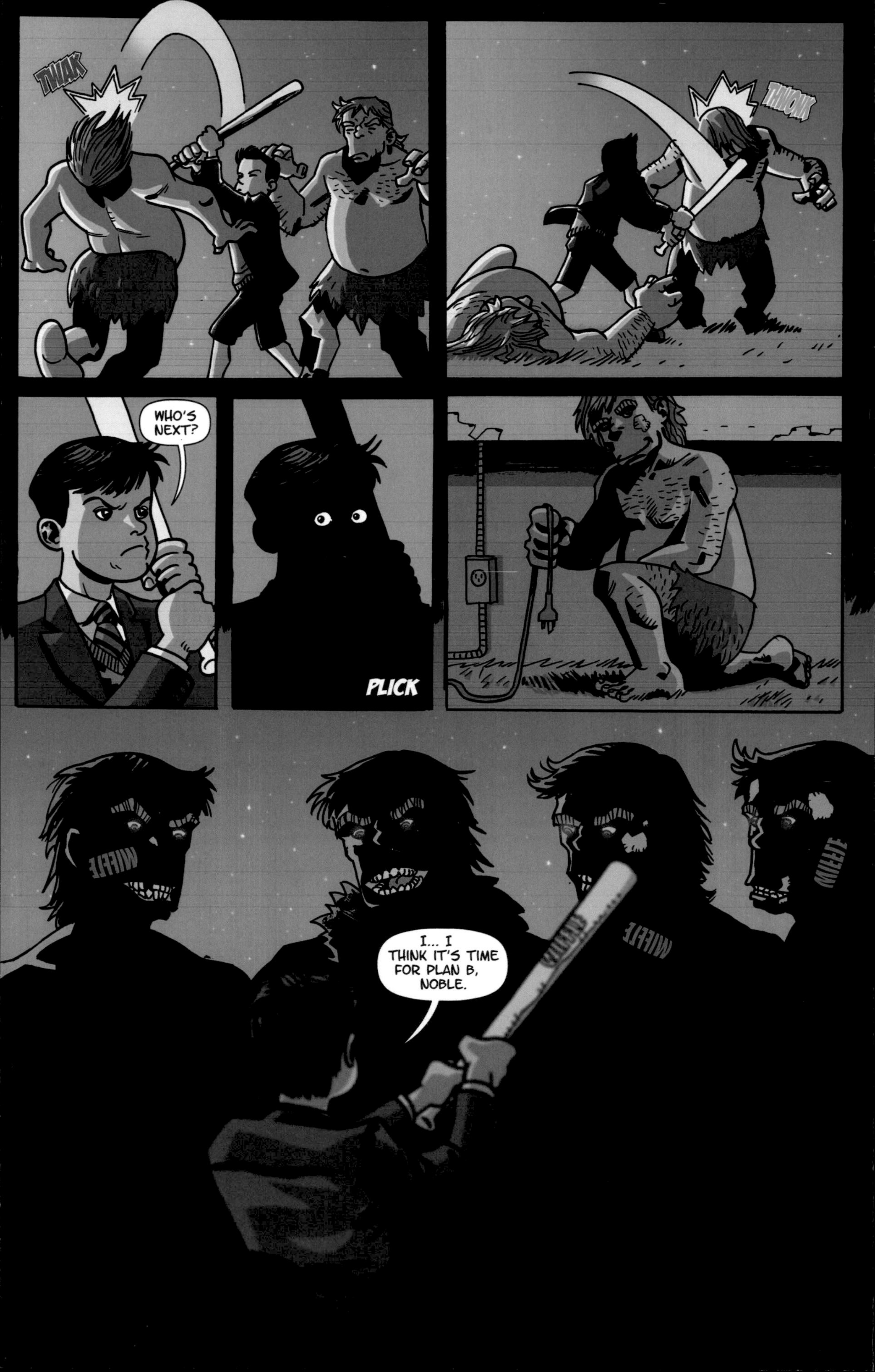
TWAK
THWONK
WHO'S NEXT?
PLICK
I... I THINK IT'S TIME FOR PLAN B, NOBLE.

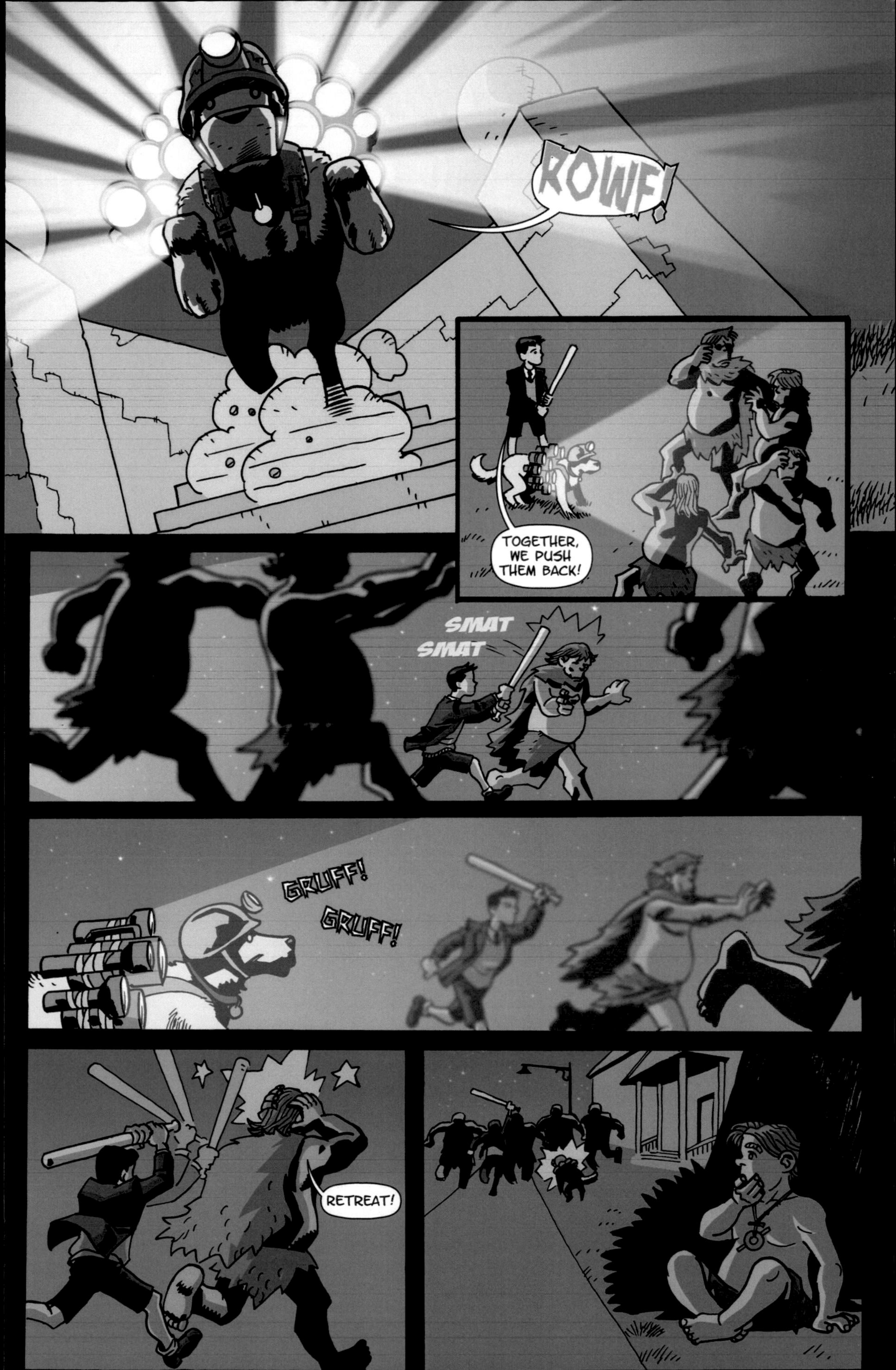
ROWF!
TOGETHER, WE PUSH THEM BACK!
SMAT
SMAT
GRUFF!
GRUFF!
RETREAT!

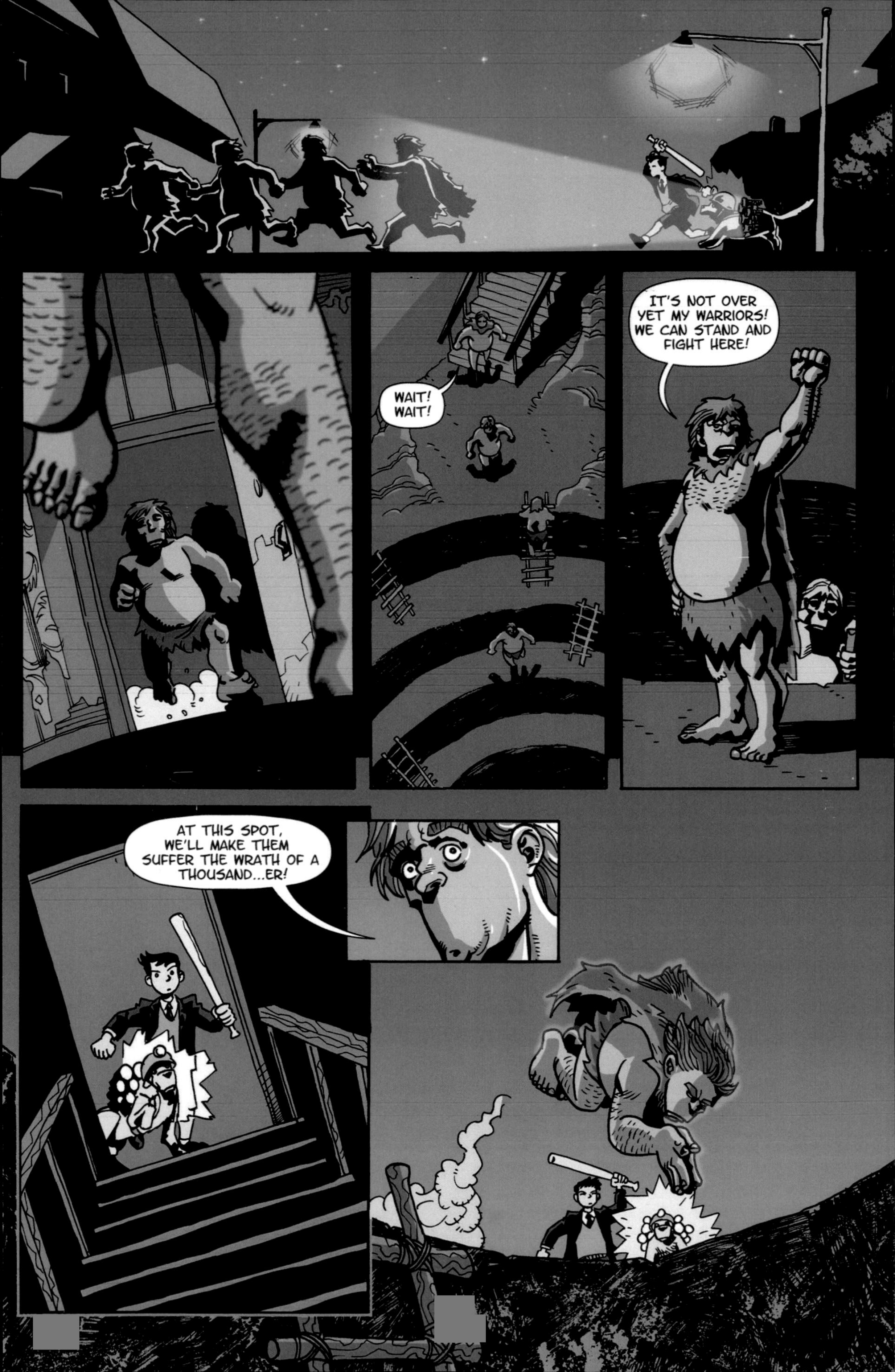
WAIT! WAIT!
IT'S NOT OVER YET MY WARRIORS! WE CAN STAND AND FIGHT HERE!
AT THIS SPOT, WE'LL MAKE THEM SUFFER THE WRATH OF A THOUSAND...ER!

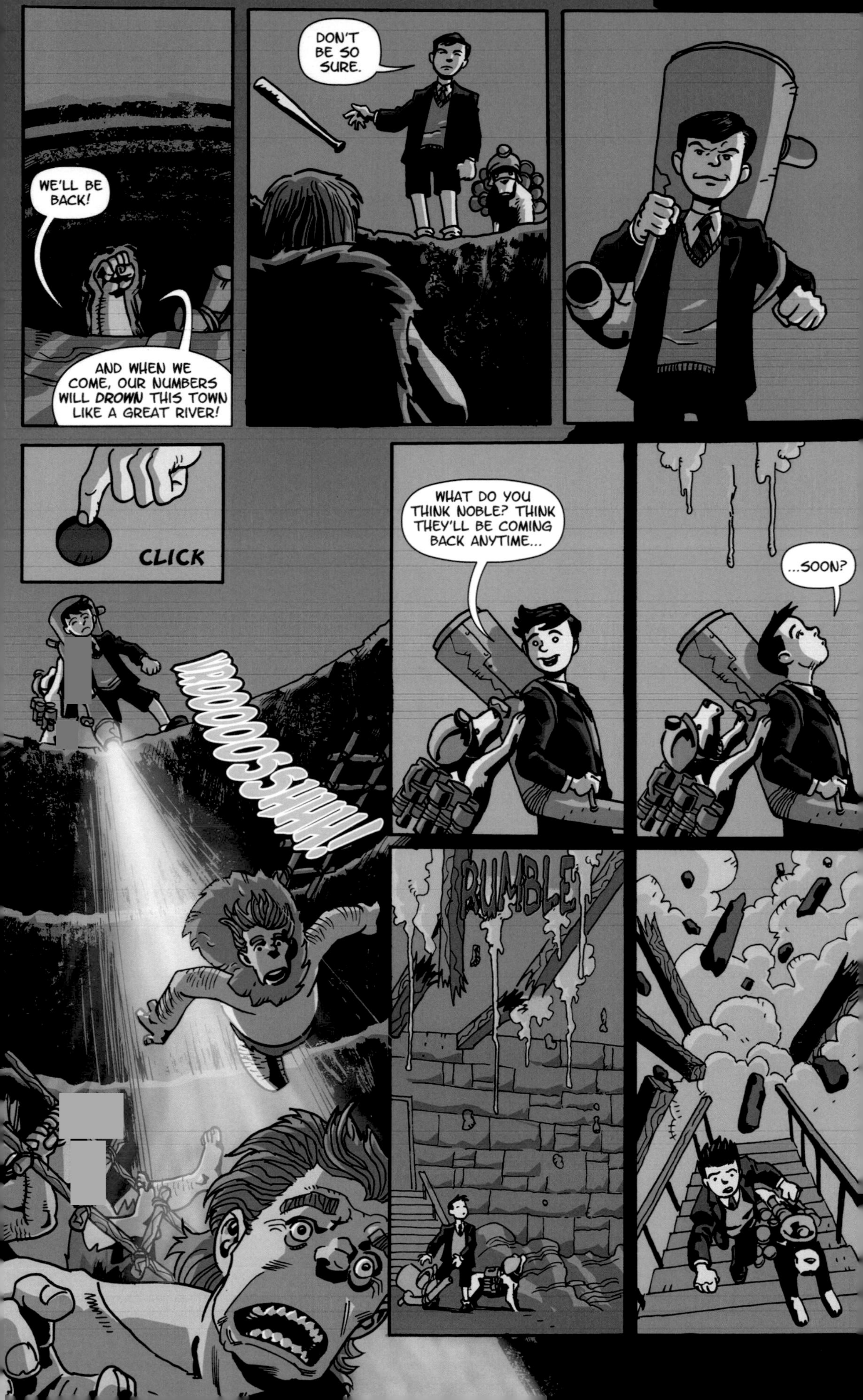

WE'LL BE BACK!
AND WHEN WE COME, OUR NUMBERS WILL *DROWN* THIS TOWN LIKE A GREAT RIVER!
DON'T BE SO SURE.
CLICK
VROOOOOSSHHH!
WHAT DO YOU THINK NOBLE? THINK THEY'LL BE COMING BACK ANYTIME...
...SOON?
RUMBLE

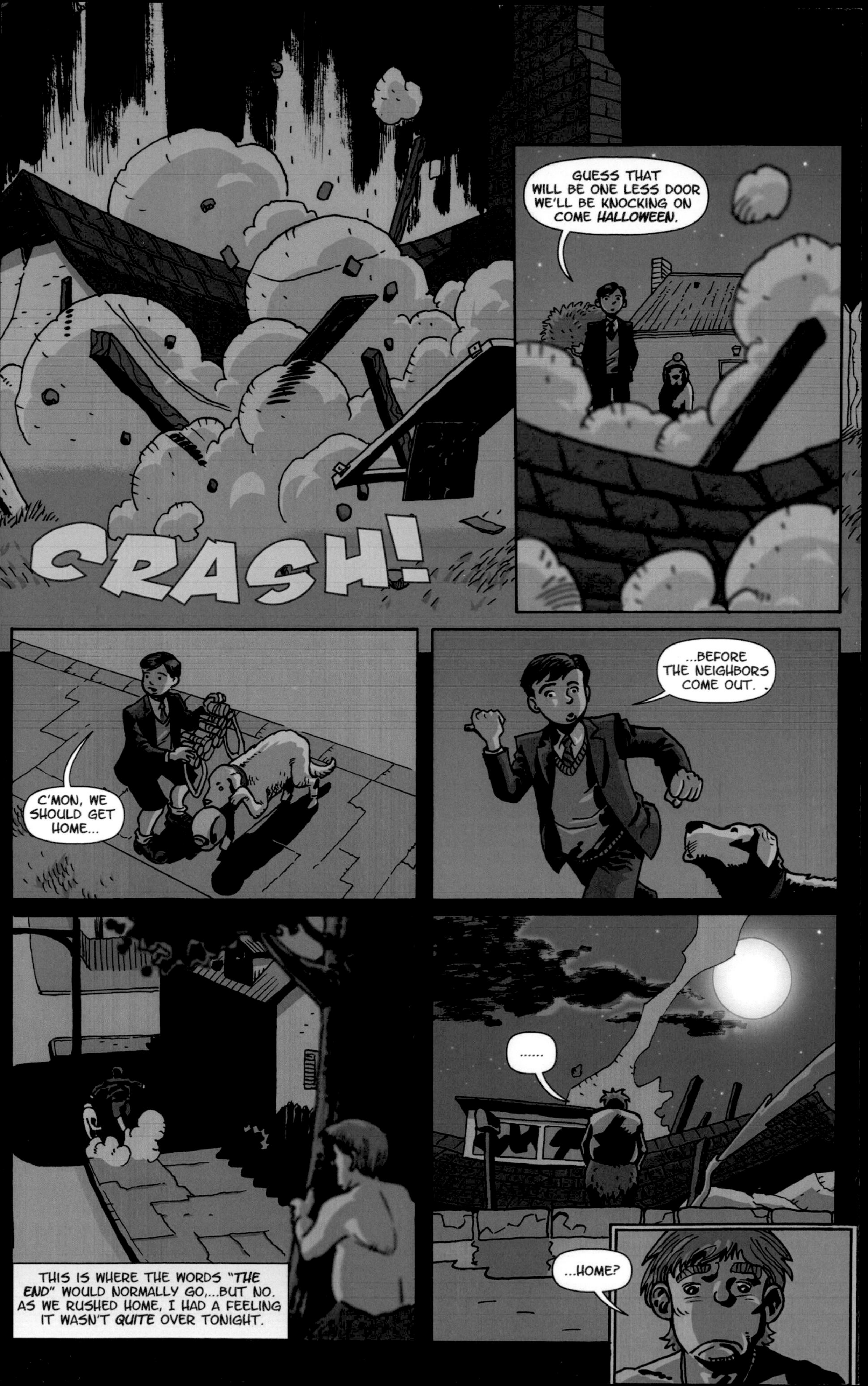
CRASH!
GUESS THAT WILL BE ONE LESS DOOR WE'LL BE KNOCKING ON COME HALLOWEEN.
C'MON, WE SHOULD GET HOME...
...BEFORE THE NEIGHBORS COME OUT.
THIS IS WHERE THE WORDS "THE END" WOULD NORMALLY GO,...BUT NO. AS WE RUSHED HOME, I HAD A FEELING IT WASN'T QUITE OVER TONIGHT.
......
...HOME?

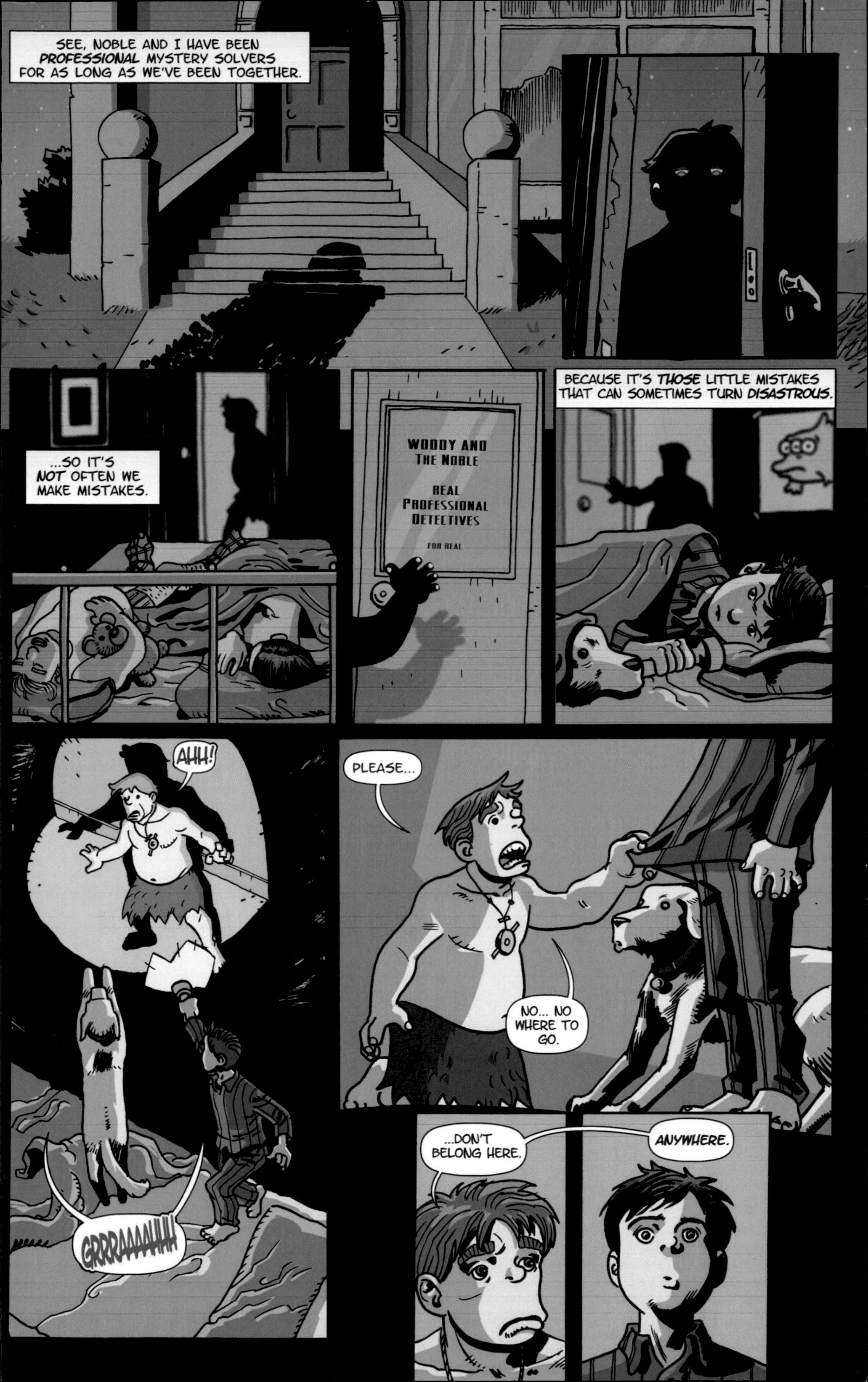
SEE, NOBLE AND I HAVE BEEN PROFESSIONAL MYSTERY SOLVERS FOR AS LONG AS WE'VE BEEN TOGETHER.
...SO IT'S NOT OFTEN WE MAKE MISTAKES.
WOODY AND THE NOBLE
REAL PROFESSIONAL DETECTIVES
FOR REAL
BECAUSE IT'S THOSE LITTLE MISTAKES THAT CAN SOMETIMES TURN DISASTROUS.
AHH!
GRRRAAAAHHH
PLEASE...
NO... NO WHERE TO GO.
...DON'T BELONG HERE.
ANYWHERE.

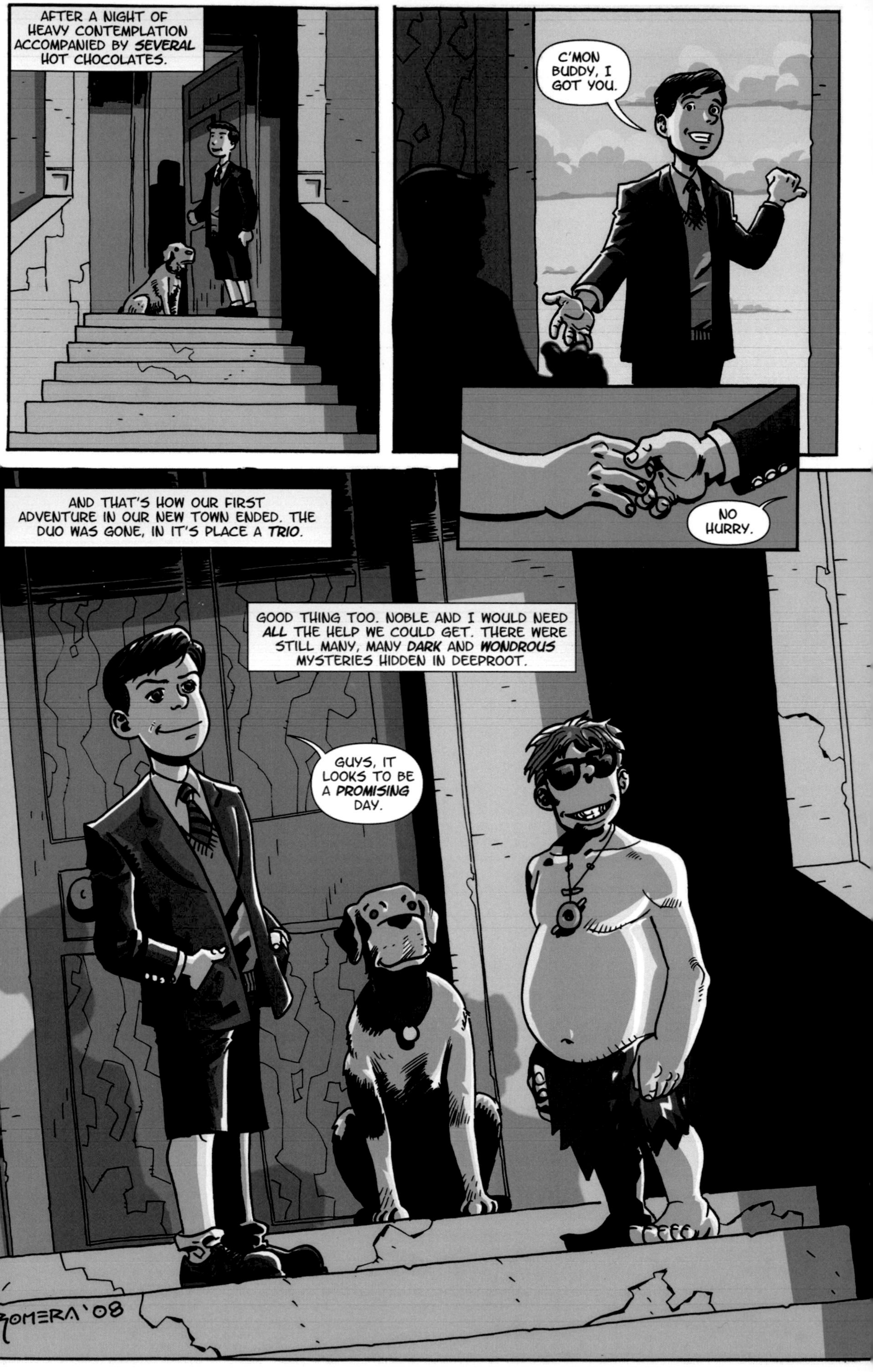
AFTER A NIGHT OF HEAVY CONTEMPLATION ACCOMPANIED BY **SEVERAL** HOT CHOCOLATES.
C'MON BUDDY, I GOT YOU.
NO HURRY.
AND THAT'S HOW OUR FIRST ADVENTURE IN OUR NEW TOWN ENDED. THE DUO WAS GONE, IN IT'S PLACE A **TRIO**.
GOOD THING TOO. NOBLE AND I WOULD NEED **ALL** THE HELP WE COULD GET. THERE WERE STILL MANY, MANY **DARK** AND **WONDROUS** MYSTERIES HIDDEN IN DEEPROOT.
GUYS, IT LOOKS TO BE A **PROMISING** DAY.
ZOMERA '08

Chapter 2

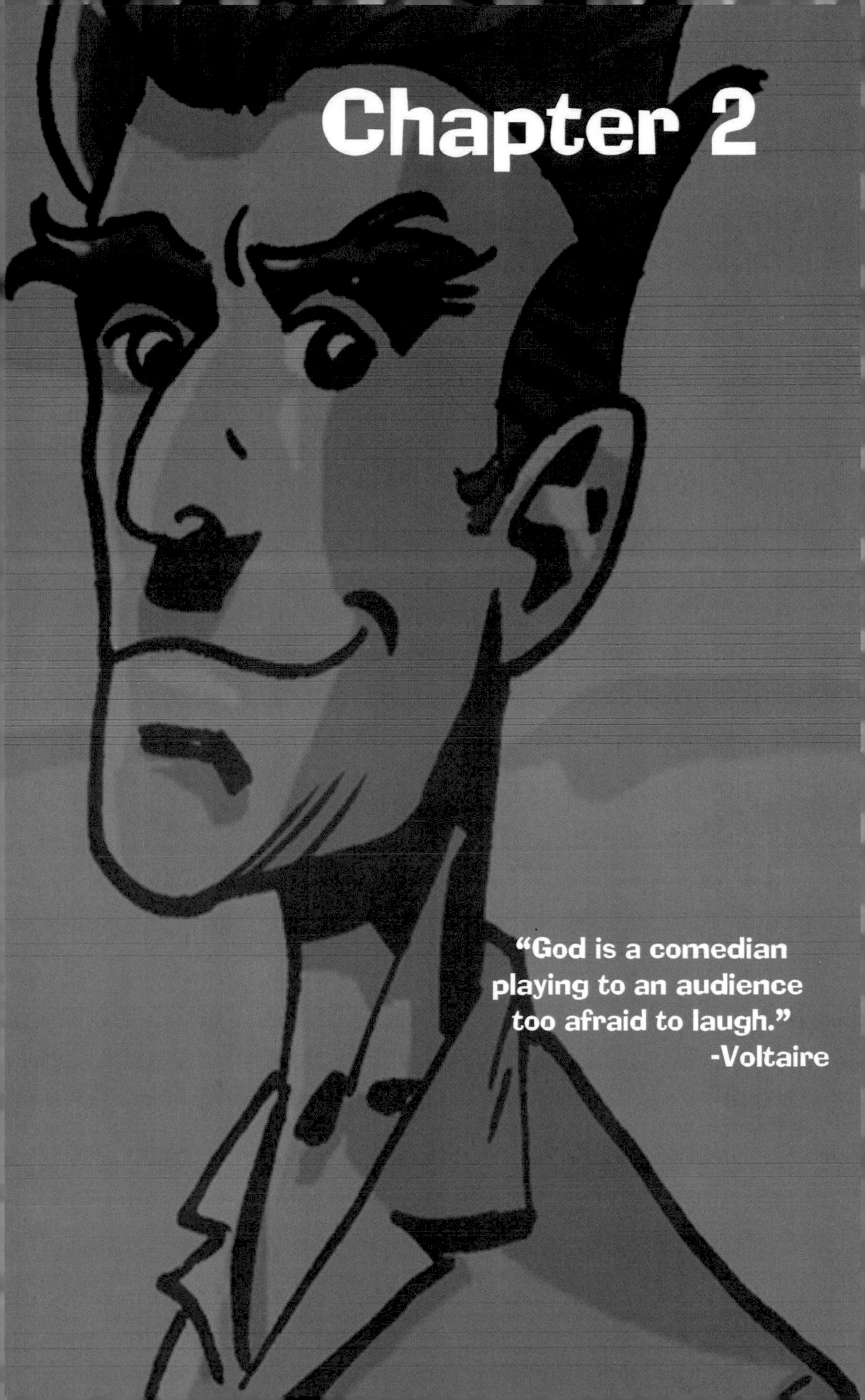

"God is a comedian playing to an audience too afraid to laugh."
-Voltaire

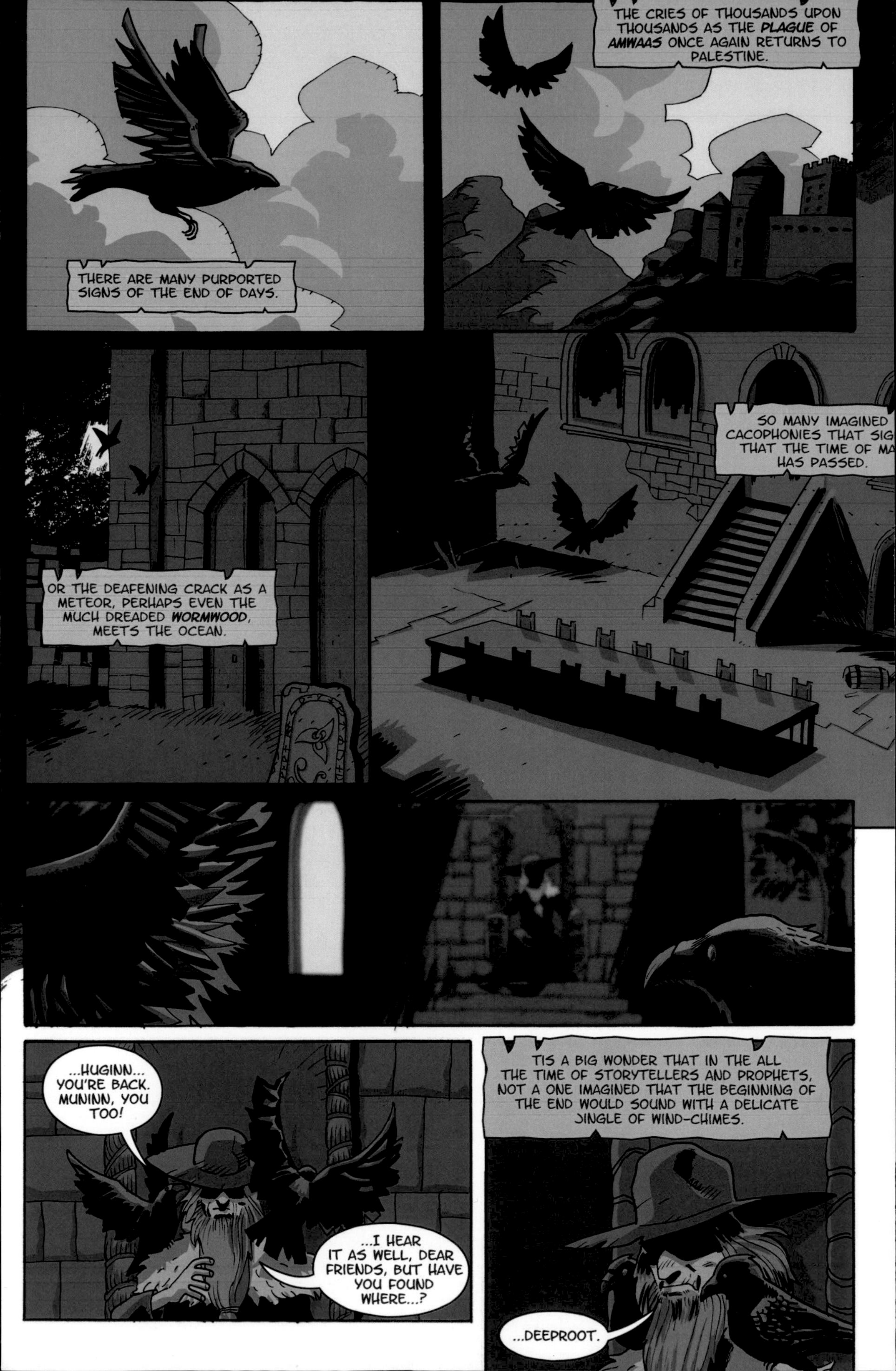
THERE ARE MANY PURPORTED SIGNS OF THE END OF DAYS.
THE CRIES OF THOUSANDS UPON THOUSANDS AS THE PLAGUE OF AMWAAS ONCE AGAIN RETURNS TO PALESTINE.
OR THE DEAFENING CRACK AS A METEOR, PERHAPS EVEN THE MUCH DREADED WORMWOOD, MEETS THE OCEAN.
SO MANY IMAGINED CACOPHONIES THAT SIG THAT THE TIME OF MA HAS PASSED.
...HUGINN... YOU'RE BACK. MUNINN, YOU TOO!
...I HEAR IT AS WELL, DEAR FRIENDS, BUT HAVE YOU FOUND WHERE...?
TIS A BIG WONDER THAT IN THE ALL THE TIME OF STORYTELLERS AND PROPHETS, NOT A ONE IMAGINED THAT THE BEGINNING OF THE END WOULD SOUND WITH A DELICATE JINGLE OF WIND-CHIMES.
...DEEPROOT.

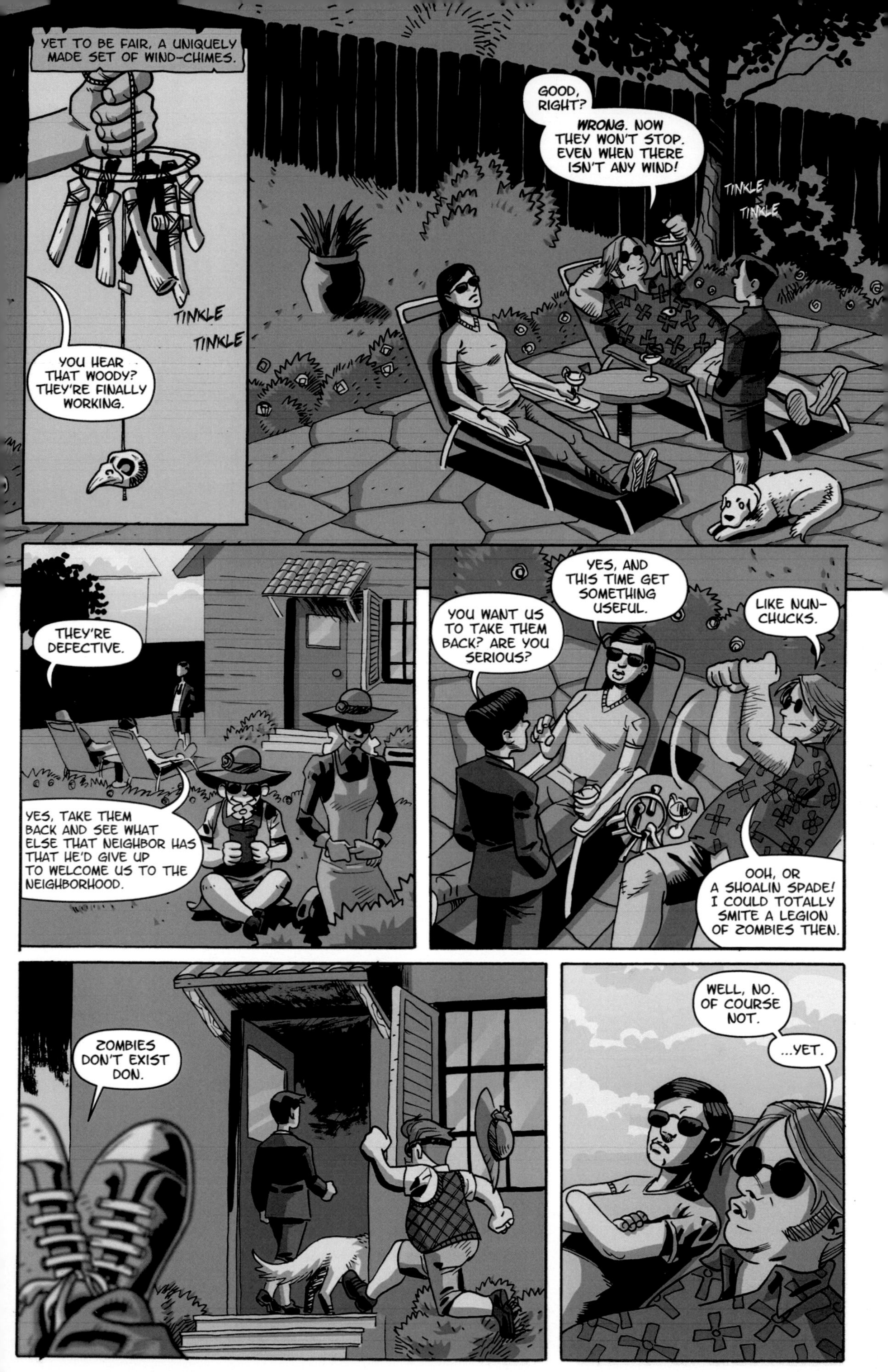
YET TO BE FAIR, A UNIQUELY MADE SET OF WIND-CHIMES.
TINKLE
TINKLE
YOU HEAR THAT WOODY? THEY'RE FINALLY WORKING.
GOOD, RIGHT?
WRONG. NOW THEY WON'T STOP. EVEN WHEN THERE ISN'T ANY WIND!
TINKLE
TINKLE
THEY'RE DEFECTIVE.
YES, TAKE THEM BACK AND SEE WHAT ELSE THAT NEIGHBOR HAS THAT HE'D GIVE UP TO WELCOME US TO THE NEIGHBORHOOD.
YOU WANT US TO TAKE THEM BACK? ARE YOU SERIOUS?
YES, AND THIS TIME GET SOMETHING USEFUL.
LIKE NUN-CHUCKS.
OOH, OR A SHOALIN SPADE! I COULD TOTALLY SMITE A LEGION OF ZOMBIES THEN.
ZOMBIES DON'T EXIST DON.
WELL, NO. OF COURSE NOT.
...YET.

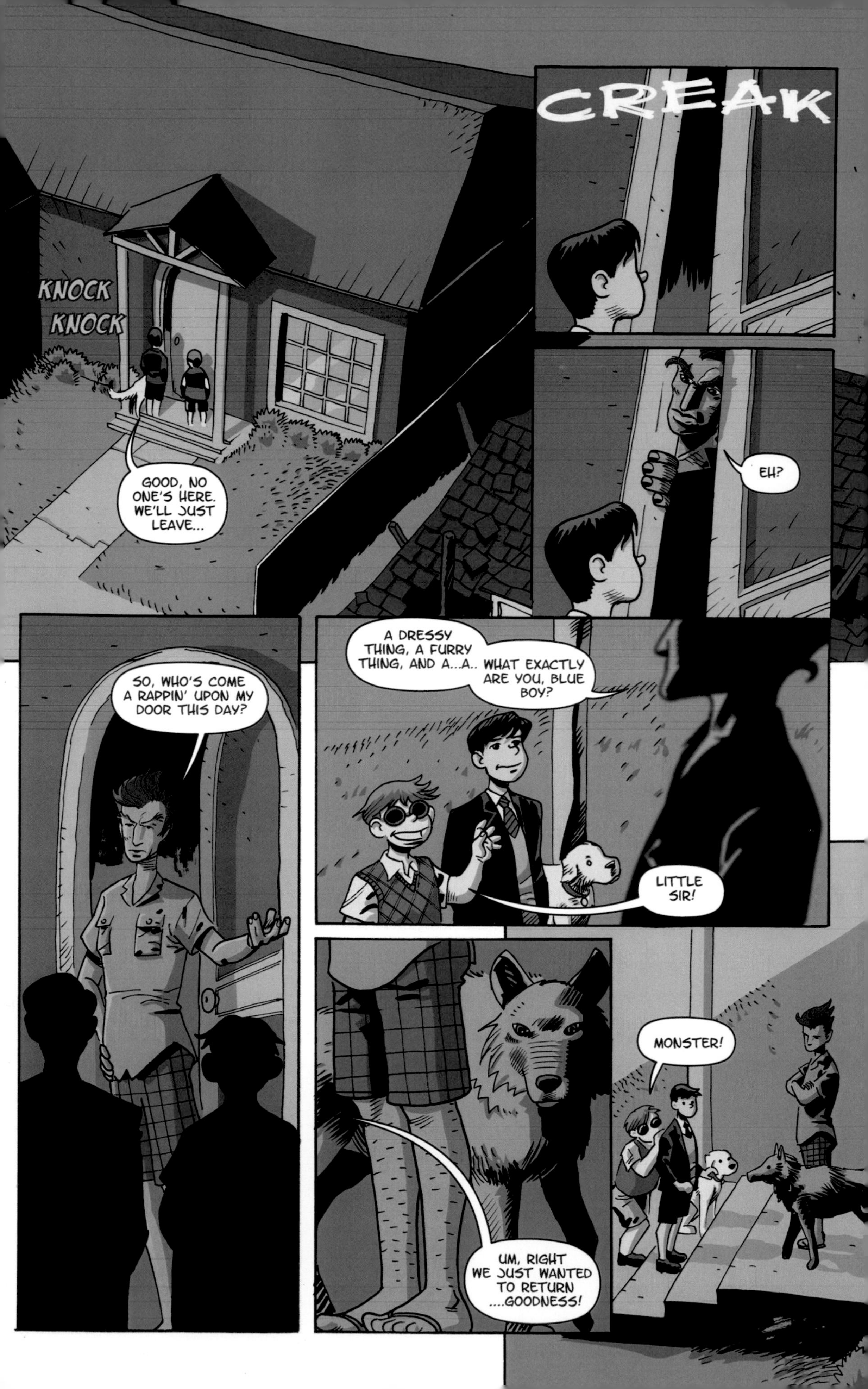
KNOCK
KNOCK
GOOD, NO ONE'S HERE. WE'LL JUST LEAVE...
CREAK
EH?
SO, WHO'S COME A RAPPIN' UPON MY DOOR THIS DAY?
A DRESSY THING, A FURRY THING, AND A...A..
WHAT EXACTLY ARE YOU, BLUE BOY?
LITTLE SIR!
UM, RIGHT WE JUST WANTED TO RETURN ....GOODNESS!
MONSTER!

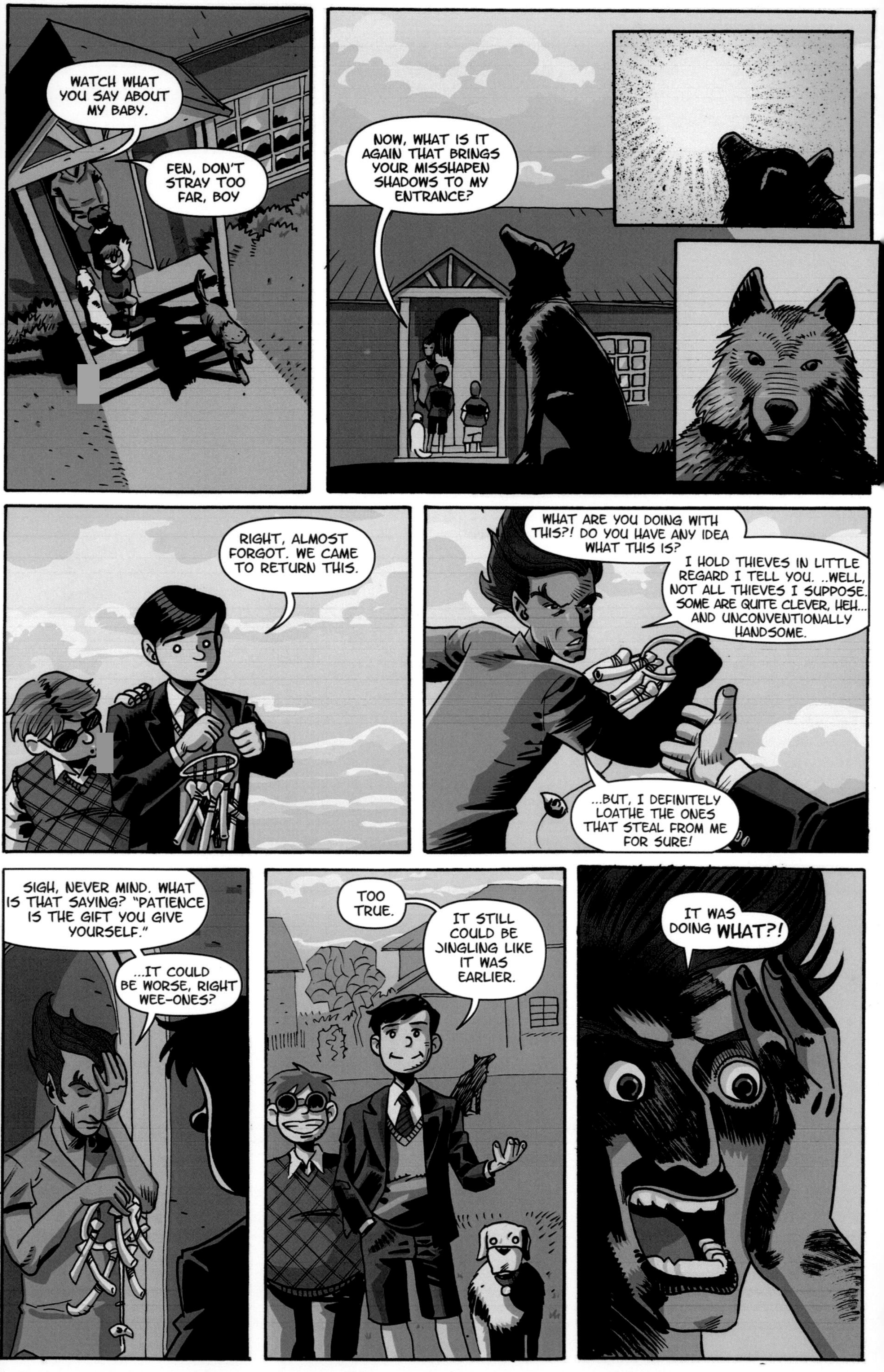
WATCH WHAT YOU SAY ABOUT MY BABY.
FEN, DON'T STRAY TOO FAR, BOY
NOW, WHAT IS IT AGAIN THAT BRINGS YOUR MISSHAPEN SHADOWS TO MY ENTRANCE?
RIGHT, ALMOST FORGOT. WE CAME TO RETURN THIS.
WHAT ARE YOU DOING WITH THIS?! DO YOU HAVE ANY IDEA WHAT THIS IS?
I HOLD THIEVES IN LITTLE REGARD I TELL YOU. ..WELL, NOT ALL THIEVES I SUPPOSE. SOME ARE QUITE CLEVER, HEH... AND UNCONVENTIONALLY HANDSOME.
...BUT, I DEFINITELY LOATHE THE ONES THAT STEAL FROM ME FOR SURE!
SIGH, NEVER MIND. WHAT IS THAT SAYING? "PATIENCE IS THE GIFT YOU GIVE YOURSELF."
...IT COULD BE WORSE, RIGHT WEE-ONES?
TOO TRUE.
IT STILL COULD BE JINGLING LIKE IT WAS EARLIER.
IT WAS DOING WHAT?!

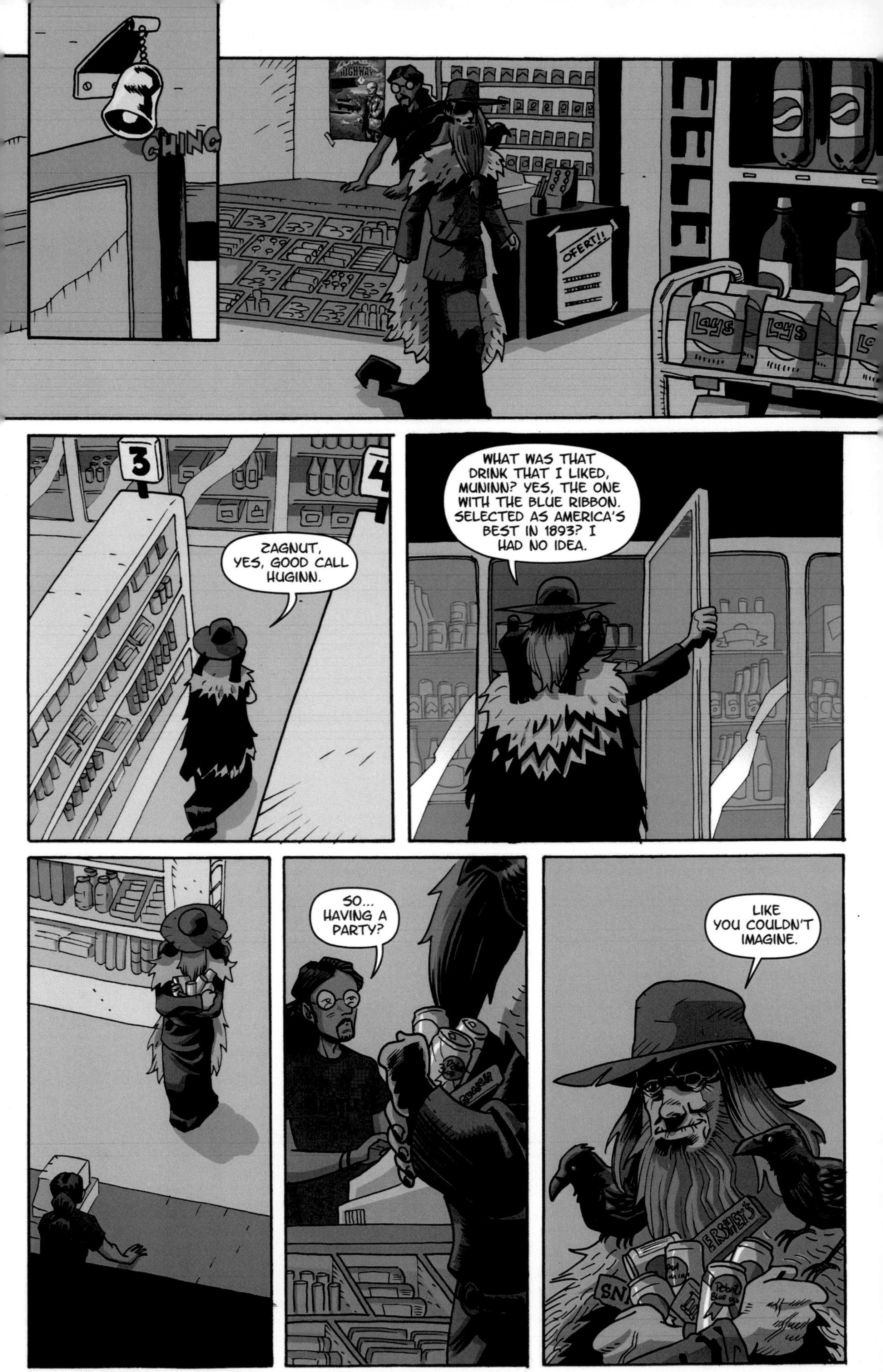
CHING
OFERT!!
ZAGNUT, YES, GOOD CALL HUGINN.
WHAT WAS THAT DRINK THAT I LIKED, MUNINN? YES, THE ONE WITH THE BLUE RIBBON. SELECTED AS AMERICA'S BEST IN 1893? I HAD NO IDEA.
SO... HAVING A PARTY?
LIKE YOU COULDN'T IMAGINE.

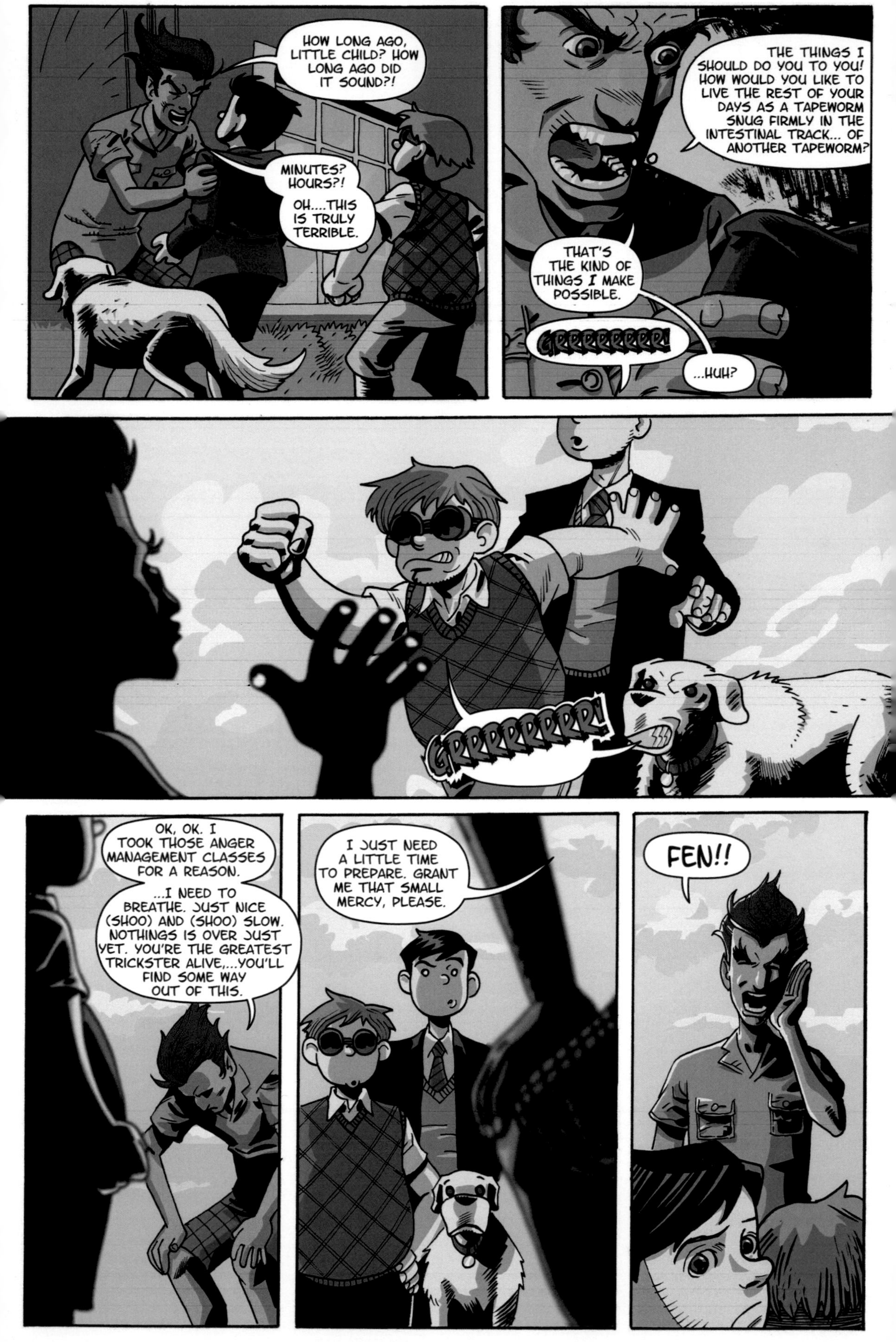
HOW LONG AGO, LITTLE CHILD? HOW LONG AGO DID IT SOUND?!
MINUTES? HOURS?!
OH....THIS IS TRULY TERRIBLE.
THE THINGS I SHOULD DO YOU TO YOU! HOW WOULD YOU LIKE TO LIVE THE REST OF YOUR DAYS AS A TAPEWORM SNUG FIRMLY IN THE INTESTINAL TRACK... OF ANOTHER TAPEWORM?
THAT'S THE KIND OF THINGS I MAKE POSSIBLE.
GRRRRRRRR!
...HUH?
GRRRRRRRR!
OK, OK. I TOOK THOSE ANGER MANAGEMENT CLASSES FOR A REASON.
...I NEED TO BREATHE. JUST NICE (SHOO) AND (SHOO) SLOW. NOTHINGS IS OVER JUST YET. YOU'RE THE GREATEST TRICKSTER ALIVE,...YOU'LL FIND SOME WAY OUT OF THIS.
I JUST NEED A LITTLE TIME TO PREPARE. GRANT ME THAT SMALL MERCY, PLEASE.
FEN!!

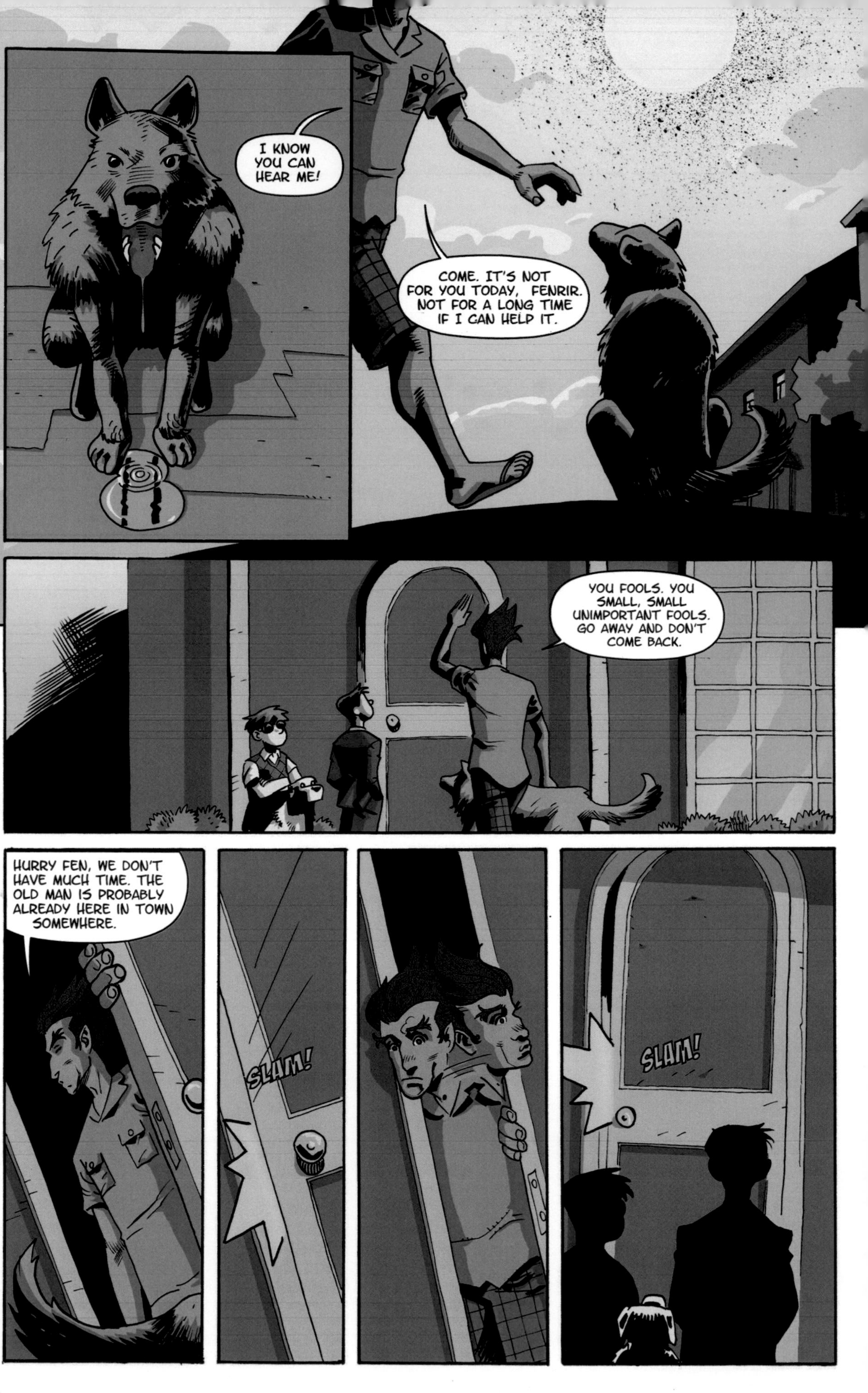
I KNOW YOU CAN HEAR ME!
COME. IT'S NOT FOR YOU TODAY, FENRIR. NOT FOR A LONG TIME IF I CAN HELP IT.
YOU FOOLS. YOU SMALL, SMALL UNIMPORTANT FOOLS. GO AWAY AND DON'T COME BACK.
HURRY FEN, WE DON'T HAVE MUCH TIME. THE OLD MAN IS PROBABLY ALREADY HERE IN TOWN SOMEWHERE.
SLAM!
SLAM!

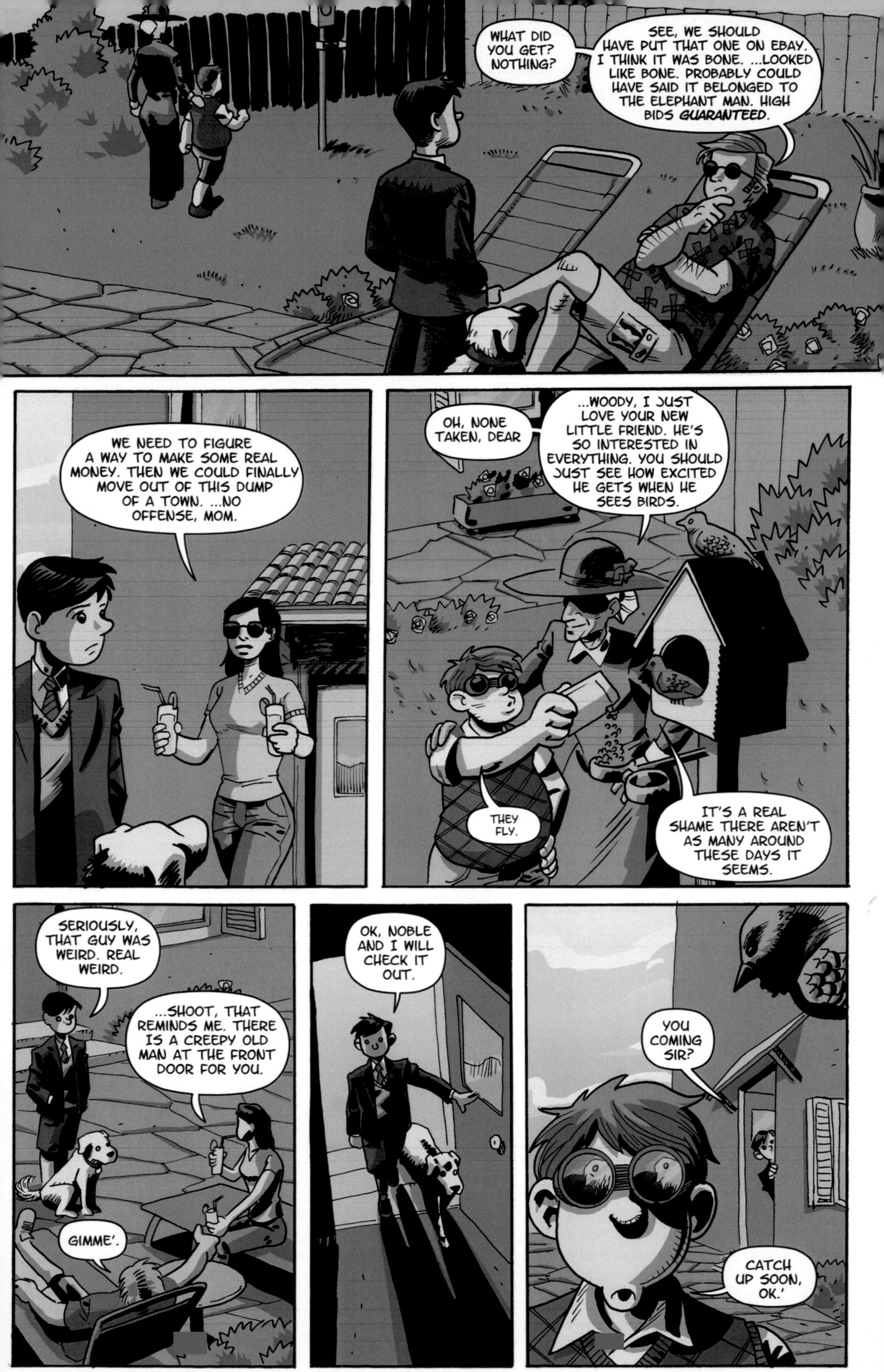
WHAT DID YOU GET? NOTHING?
SEE, WE SHOULD HAVE PUT THAT ONE ON EBAY. I THINK IT WAS BONE. ...LOOKED LIKE BONE. PROBABLY COULD HAVE SAID IT BELONGED TO THE ELEPHANT MAN. HIGH BIDS GUARANTEED.
WE NEED TO FIGURE A WAY TO MAKE SOME REAL MONEY. THEN WE COULD FINALLY MOVE OUT OF THIS DUMP OF A TOWN. ...NO OFFENSE, MOM.
OH, NONE TAKEN, DEAR
...WOODY, I JUST LOVE YOUR NEW LITTLE FRIEND. HE'S SO INTERESTED IN EVERYTHING. YOU SHOULD JUST SEE HOW EXCITED HE GETS WHEN HE SEES BIRDS.
THEY FLY.
IT'S A REAL SHAME THERE AREN'T AS MANY AROUND THESE DAYS IT SEEMS.
SERIOUSLY, THAT GUY WAS WEIRD. REAL WEIRD.
...SHOOT, THAT REMINDS ME. THERE IS A CREEPY OLD MAN AT THE FRONT DOOR FOR YOU.
GIMME'.
OK, NOBLE AND I WILL CHECK IT OUT.
YOU COMING SIR?
CATCH UP SOON, OK.'

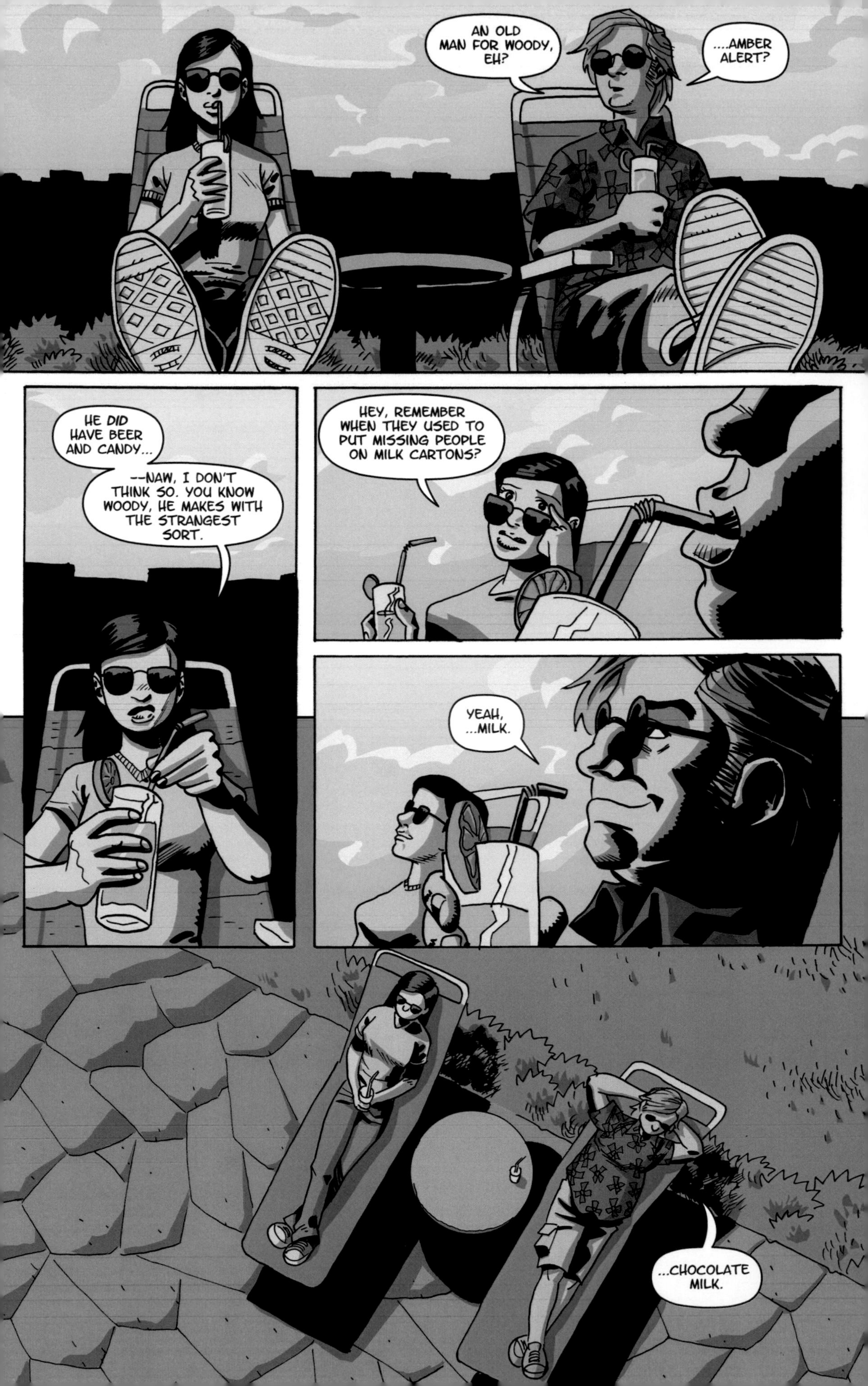
AN OLD MAN FOR WOODY, EH?
....AMBER ALERT?
HE DID HAVE BEER AND CANDY...
--NAW, I DON'T THINK SO. YOU KNOW WOODY, HE MAKES WITH THE STRANGEST SORT.
HEY, REMEMBER WHEN THEY USED TO PUT MISSING PEOPLE ON MILK CARTONS?
YEAH, ...MILK.
...CHOCOLATE MILK.

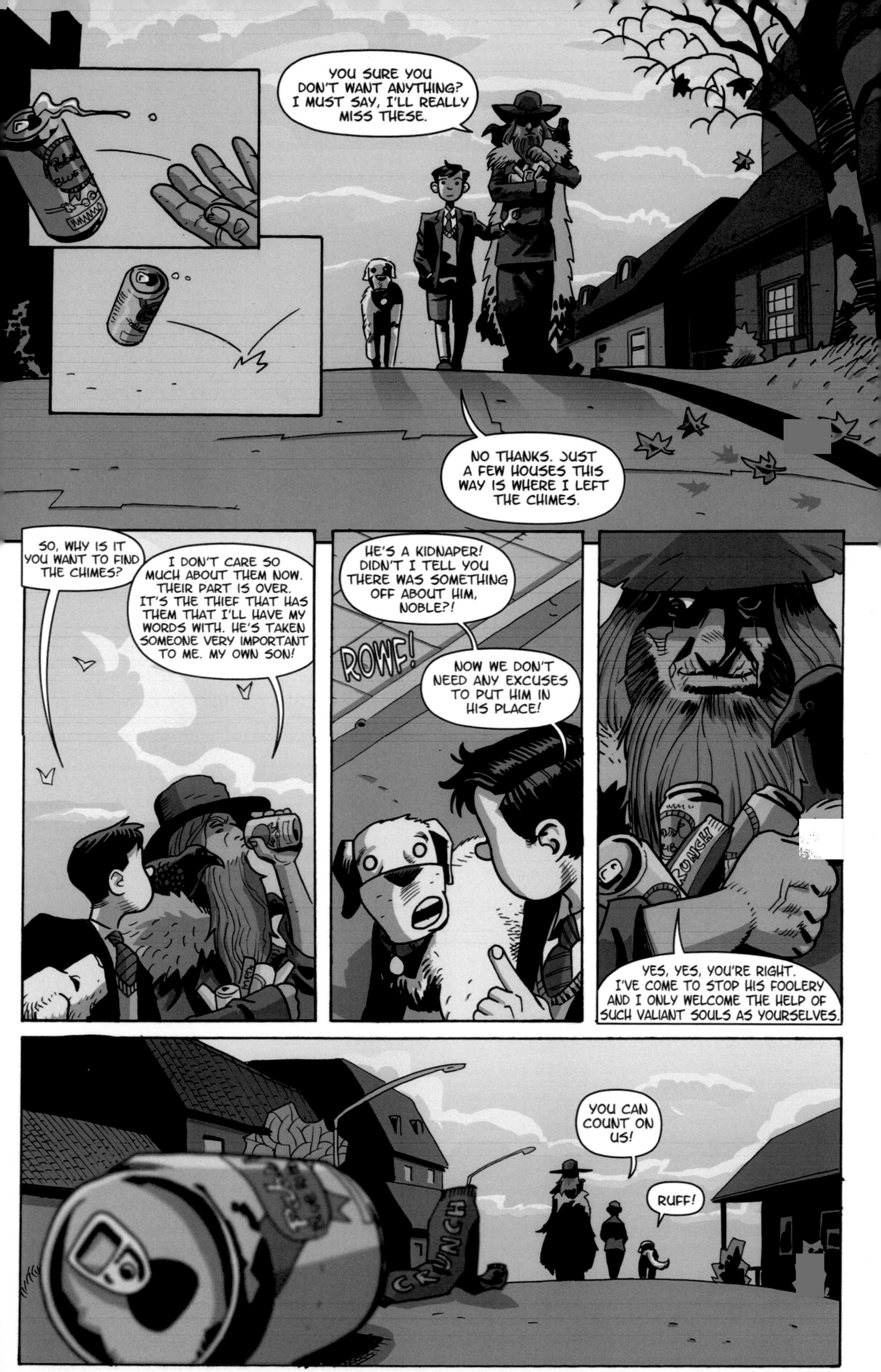
YOU SURE YOU DON'T WANT ANYTHING? I MUST SAY, I'LL REALLY MISS THESE.
NO THANKS. JUST A FEW HOUSES THIS WAY IS WHERE I LEFT THE CHIMES.
SO, WHY IS IT YOU WANT TO FIND THE CHIMES?
I DON'T CARE SO MUCH ABOUT THEM NOW. THEIR PART IS OVER. IT'S THE THIEF THAT HAS THEM THAT I'LL HAVE MY WORDS WITH. HE'S TAKEN SOMEONE VERY IMPORTANT TO ME. MY OWN SON!
HE'S A KIDNAPER! DIDN'T I TELL YOU THERE WAS SOMETHING OFF ABOUT HIM, NOBLE?!
ROWF!
NOW WE DON'T NEED ANY EXCUSES TO PUT HIM IN HIS PLACE!
YES, YES, YOU'RE RIGHT. I'VE COME TO STOP HIS FOOLERY AND I ONLY WELCOME THE HELP OF SUCH VALIANT SOULS AS YOURSELVES.
YOU CAN COUNT ON US!
RUFF!
CRUNCH

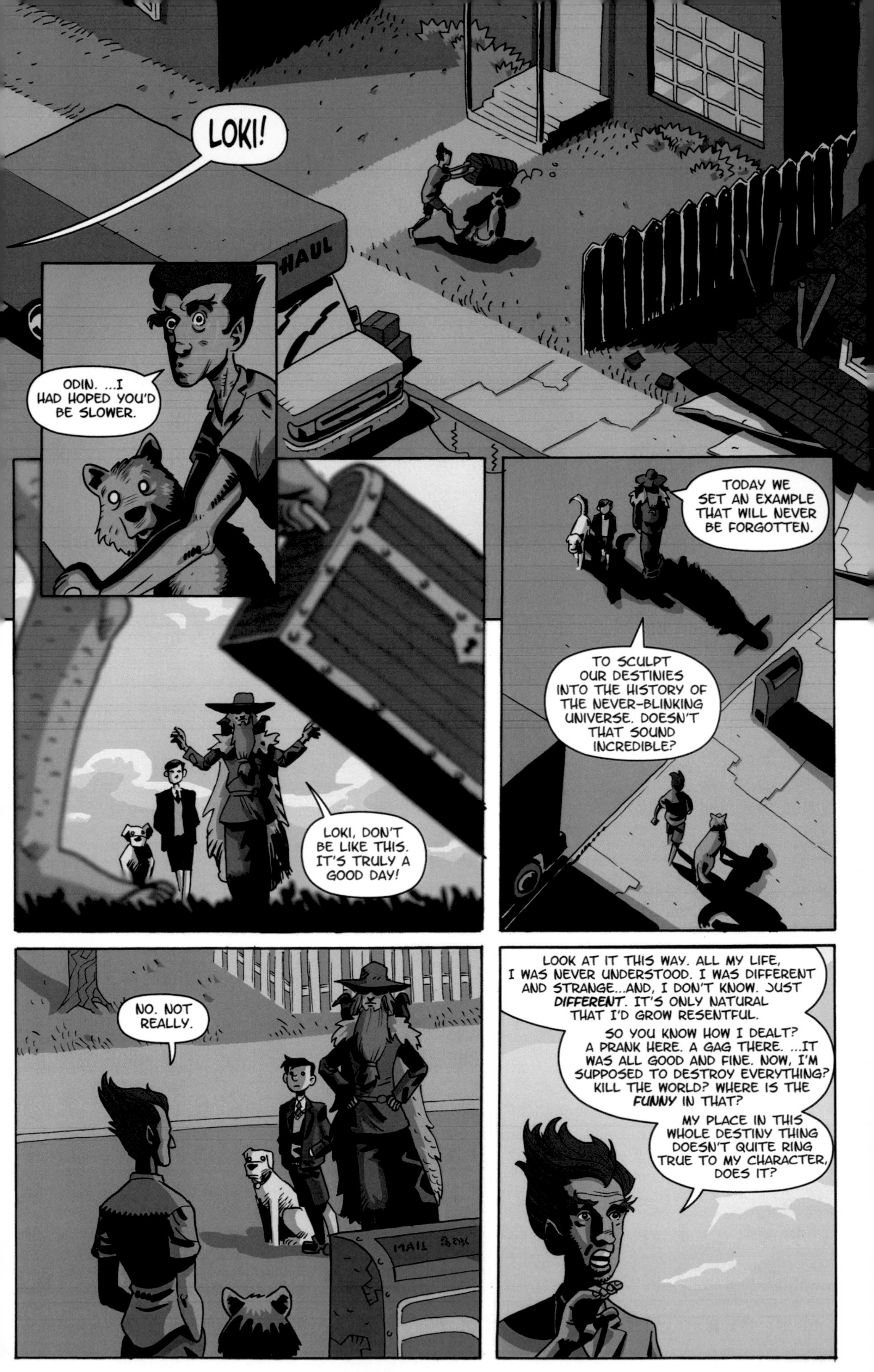
LOKI!
HAUL
ODIN. ...I HAD HOPED YOU'D BE SLOWER.
TODAY WE SET AN EXAMPLE THAT WILL NEVER BE FORGOTTEN.
TO SCULPT OUR DESTINIES INTO THE HISTORY OF THE NEVER-BLINKING UNIVERSE. DOESN'T THAT SOUND INCREDIBLE?
LOKI, DON'T BE LIKE THIS. IT'S TRULY A GOOD DAY!
NO. NOT REALLY.
MAIL
LOOK AT IT THIS WAY. ALL MY LIFE, I WAS NEVER UNDERSTOOD. I WAS DIFFERENT AND STRANGE...AND, I DON'T KNOW. JUST *DIFFERENT*. IT'S ONLY NATURAL THAT I'D GROW RESENTFUL.
SO YOU KNOW HOW I DEALT? A PRANK HERE. A GAG THERE. ...IT WAS ALL GOOD AND FINE. NOW, I'M SUPPOSED TO DESTROY EVERYTHING? KILL THE WORLD? WHERE IS THE *FUNNY* IN THAT?
MY PLACE IN THIS WHOLE DESTINY THING DOESN'T QUITE RING TRUE TO MY CHARACTER, DOES IT?

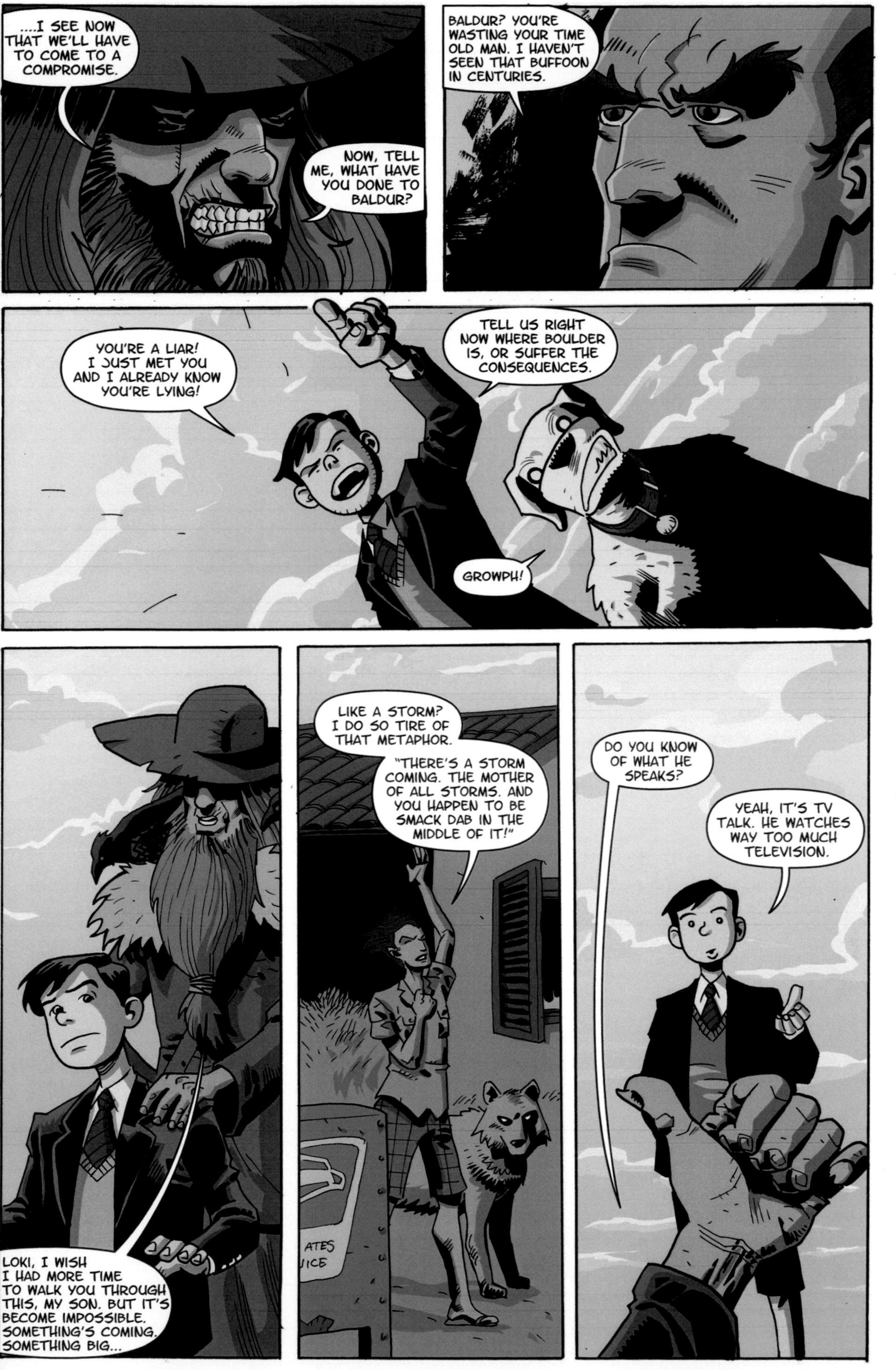

....I SEE NOW THAT WE'LL HAVE TO COME TO A COMPROMISE.
NOW, TELL ME, WHAT HAVE YOU DONE TO BALDUR?
BALDUR? YOU'RE WASTING YOUR TIME OLD MAN. I HAVEN'T SEEN THAT BUFFOON IN CENTURIES.
YOU'RE A LIAR! I JUST MET YOU AND I ALREADY KNOW YOU'RE LYING!
TELL US RIGHT NOW WHERE BOULDER IS, OR SUFFER THE CONSEQUENCES.
GROWPH!
LOKI, I WISH I HAD MORE TIME TO WALK YOU THROUGH THIS, MY SON. BUT IT'S BECOME IMPOSSIBLE. SOMETHING'S COMING. SOMETHING BIG...
LIKE A STORM? I DO SO TIRE OF THAT METAPHOR.
"THERE'S A STORM COMING. THE MOTHER OF ALL STORMS. AND YOU HAPPEN TO BE SMACK DAB IN THE MIDDLE OF IT!"
DO YOU KNOW OF WHAT HE SPEAKS?
YEAH, IT'S TV TALK. HE WATCHES WAY TOO MUCH TELEVISION.

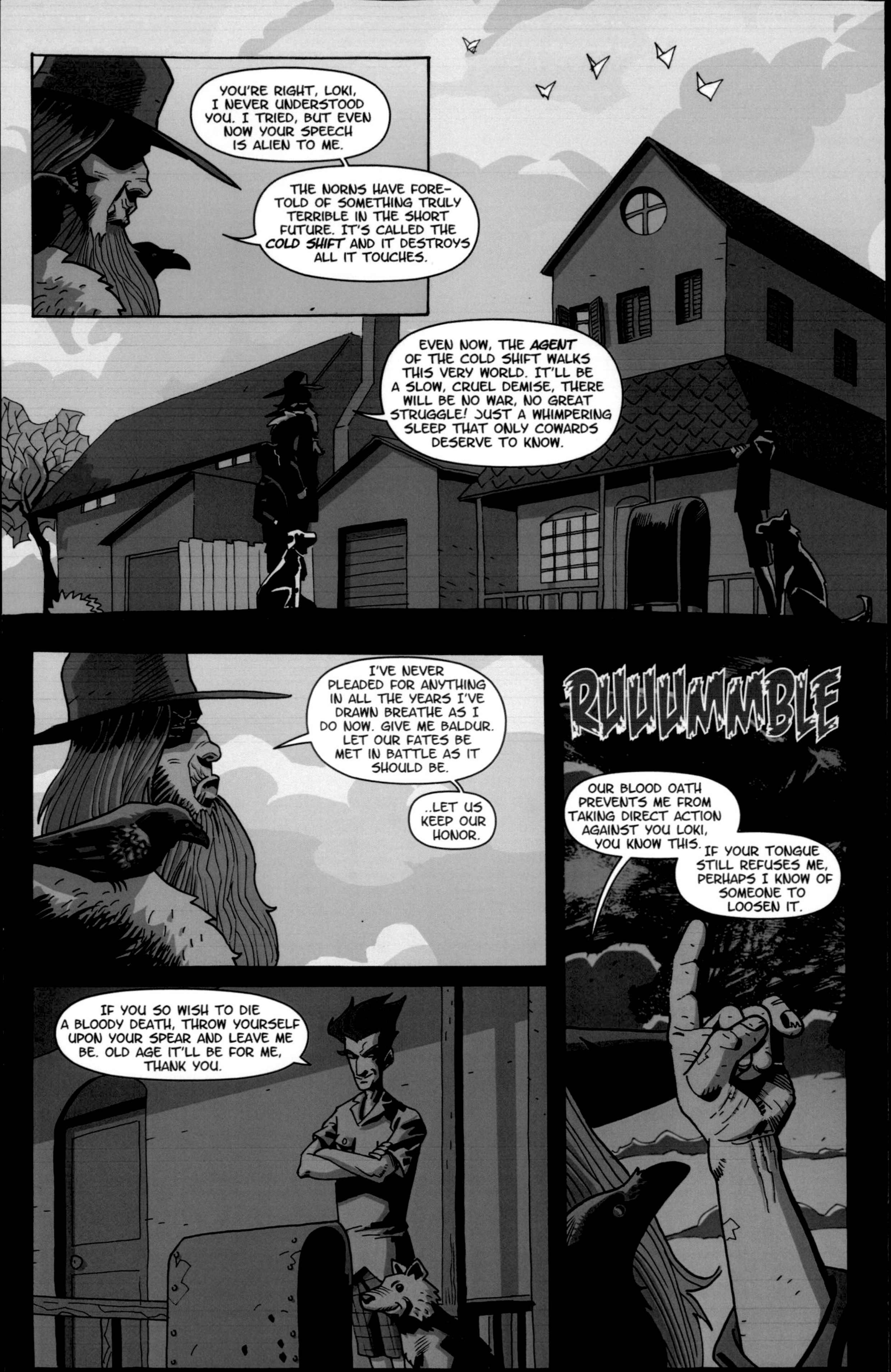
YOU'RE RIGHT, LOKI, I NEVER UNDERSTOOD YOU. I TRIED, BUT EVEN NOW YOUR SPEECH IS ALIEN TO ME.
THE NORNS HAVE FORE-TOLD OF SOMETHING TRULY TERRIBLE IN THE SHORT FUTURE. IT'S CALLED THE COLD SHIFT AND IT DESTROYS ALL IT TOUCHES.
EVEN NOW, THE AGENT OF THE COLD SHIFT WALKS THIS VERY WORLD. IT'LL BE A SLOW, CRUEL DEMISE, THERE WILL BE NO WAR, NO GREAT STRUGGLE! JUST A WHIMPERING SLEEP THAT ONLY COWARDS DESERVE TO KNOW.
I'VE NEVER PLEADED FOR ANYTHING IN ALL THE YEARS I'VE DRAWN BREATHE AS I DO NOW. GIVE ME BALDUR. LET OUR FATES BE MET IN BATTLE AS IT SHOULD BE.
..LET US KEEP OUR HONOR.
IF YOU SO WISH TO DIE A BLOODY DEATH, THROW YOURSELF UPON YOUR SPEAR AND LEAVE ME BE. OLD AGE IT'LL BE FOR ME, THANK YOU.
RUUUMMBLE
OUR BLOOD OATH PREVENTS ME FROM TAKING DIRECT ACTION AGAINST YOU LOKI, YOU KNOW THIS.
IF YOUR TONGUE STILL REFUSES ME, PERHAPS I KNOW OF SOMEONE TO LOOSEN IT.

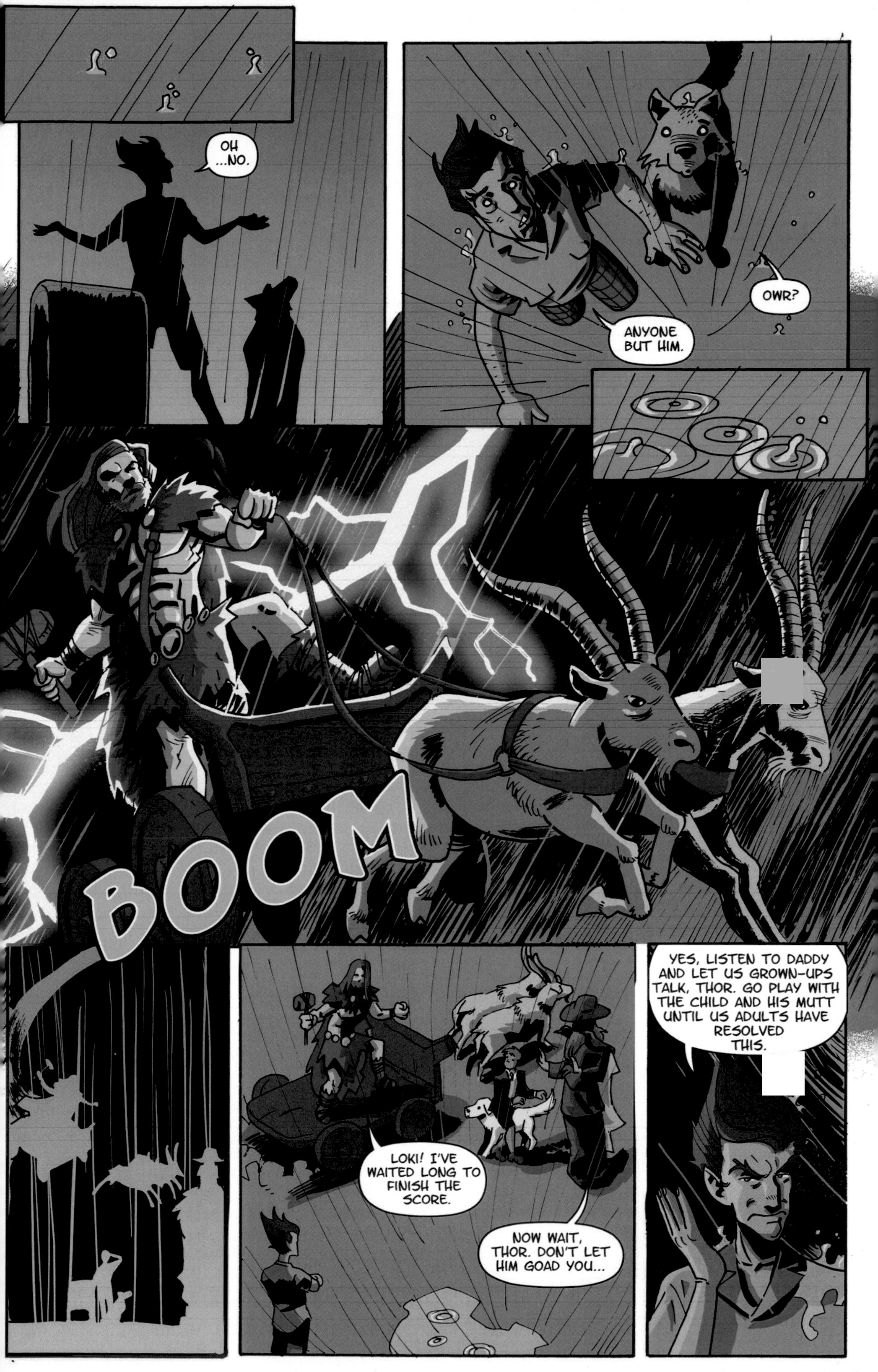
OH ...NO.
ANYONE BUT HIM.
OWR?
BOOM
LOKI! I'VE WAITED LONG TO FINISH THE SCORE.
NOW WAIT, THOR. DON'T LET HIM GOAD YOU...
YES, LISTEN TO DADDY AND LET US GROWN-UPS TALK, THOR. GO PLAY WITH THE CHILD AND HIS MUTT UNTIL US ADULTS HAVE RESOLVED THIS.

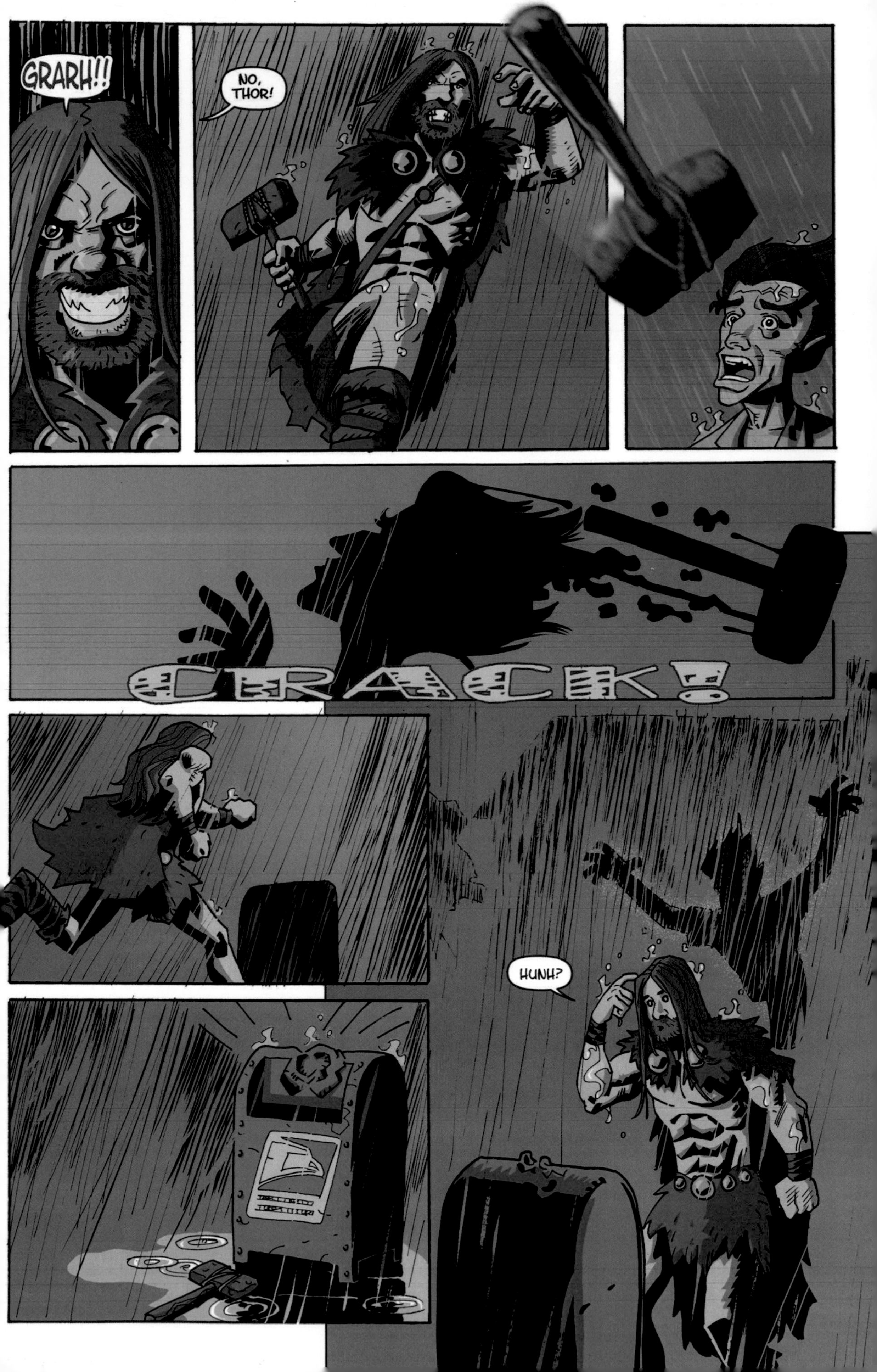
GRARH!!
NO, THOR!
CRACK!
HUNH?

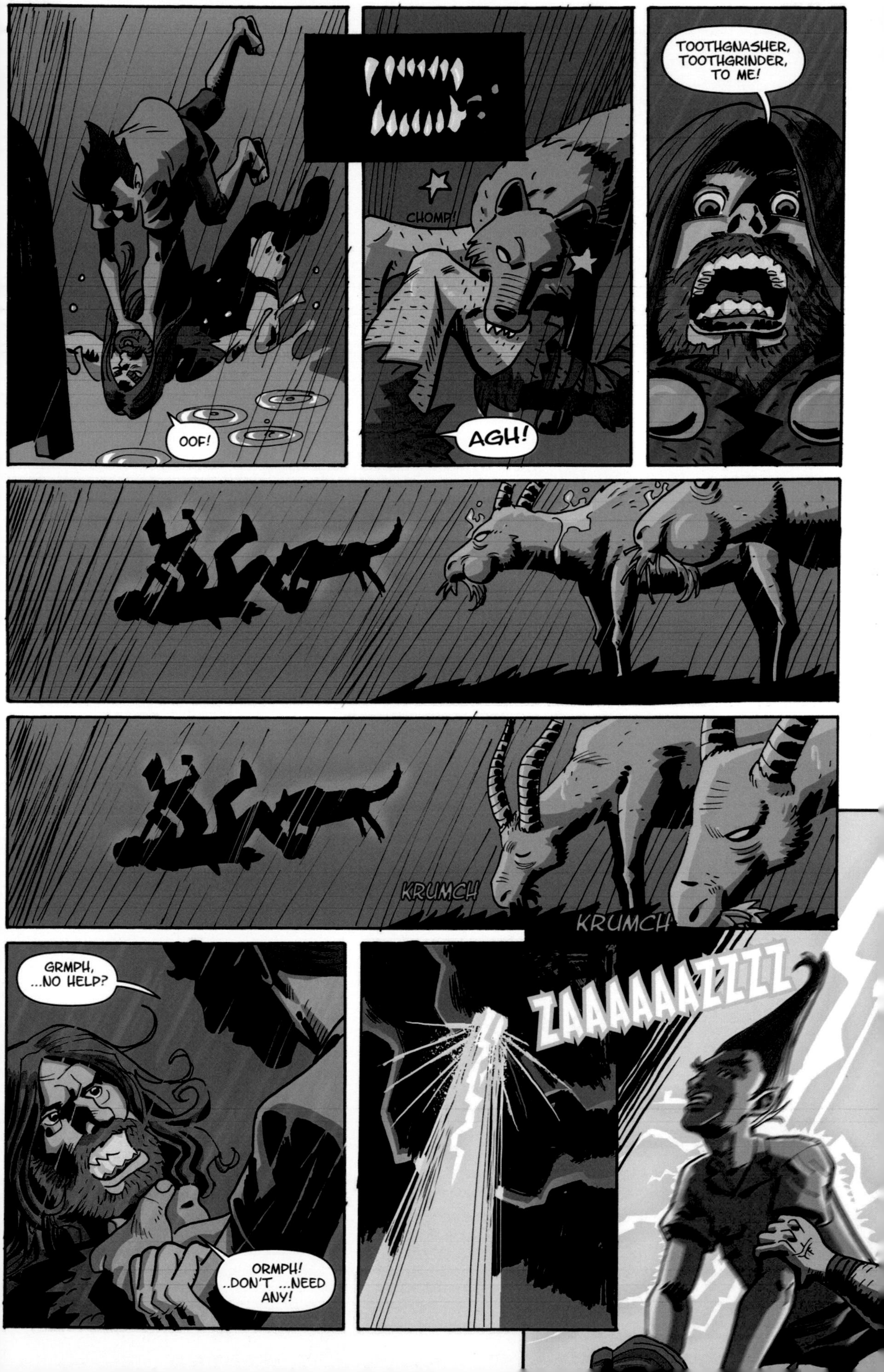
OOF!
CHOMP!
AGH!
TOOTHGNASHER, TOOTHGRINDER, TO ME!
KRUMCH
KRUMCH
GRMPH, ...NO HELP?
ORMPH! ..DON'T ...NEED ANY!
ZAAAAAAZZZZ

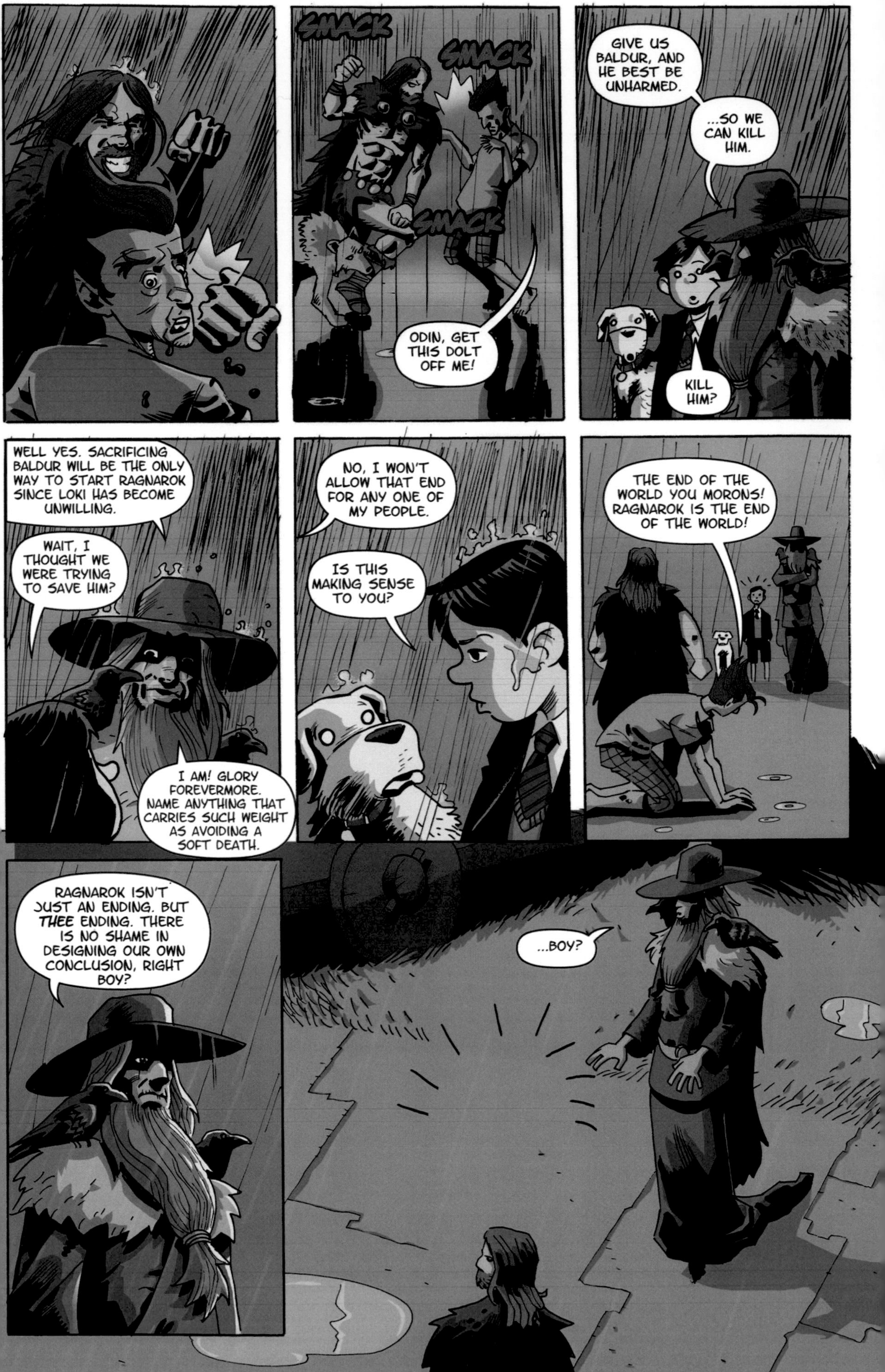
SMACK
SMACK
SMACK
ODIN, GET THIS DOLT OFF ME!
GIVE US BALDUR, AND HE BEST BE UNHARMED.
...SO WE CAN KILL HIM.
KILL HIM?
WELL YES. SACRIFICING BALDUR WILL BE THE ONLY WAY TO START RAGNAROK SINCE LOKI HAS BECOME UNWILLING.
WAIT, I THOUGHT WE WERE TRYING TO SAVE HIM?
I AM! GLORY FOREVERMORE. NAME ANYTHING THAT CARRIES SUCH WEIGHT AS AVOIDING A SOFT DEATH.
NO, I WON'T ALLOW THAT END FOR ANY ONE OF MY PEOPLE.
IS THIS MAKING SENSE TO YOU?
THE END OF THE WORLD YOU MORONS! RAGNAROK IS THE END OF THE WORLD!
RAGNAROK ISN'T JUST AN ENDING. BUT THEE ENDING. THERE IS NO SHAME IN DESIGNING OUR OWN CONCLUSION, RIGHT BOY?
...BOY?

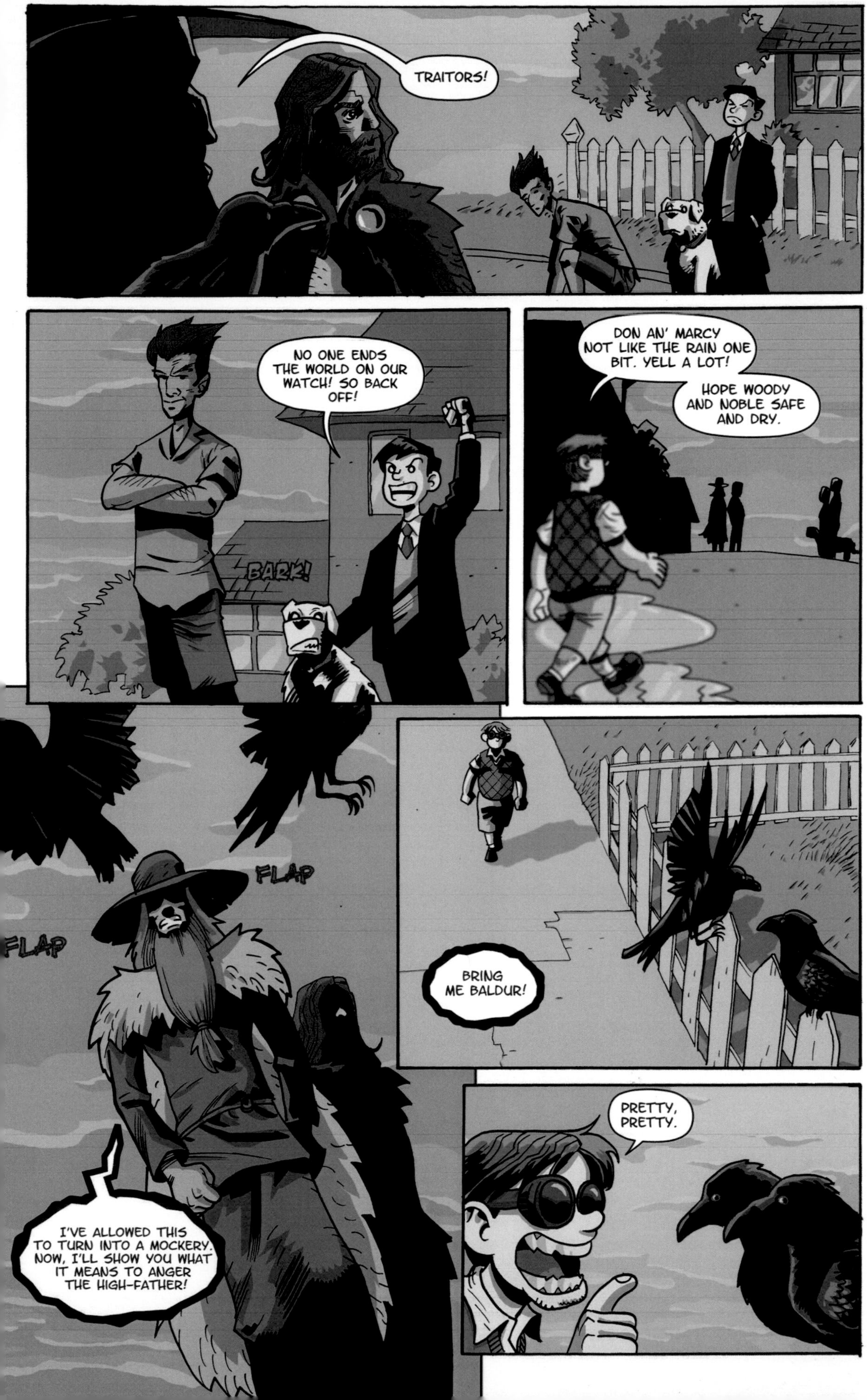
TRAITORS!
NO ONE ENDS THE WORLD ON OUR WATCH! SO BACK OFF!
BARK!
DON AN' MARCY NOT LIKE THE RAIN ONE BIT. YELL A LOT!
HOPE WOODY AND NOBLE SAFE AND DRY.
FLAP
FLAP
I'VE ALLOWED THIS TO TURN INTO A MOCKERY. NOW, I'LL SHOW YOU WHAT IT MEANS TO ANGER THE HIGH-FATHER!
BRING ME BALDUR!
PRETTY, PRETTY.

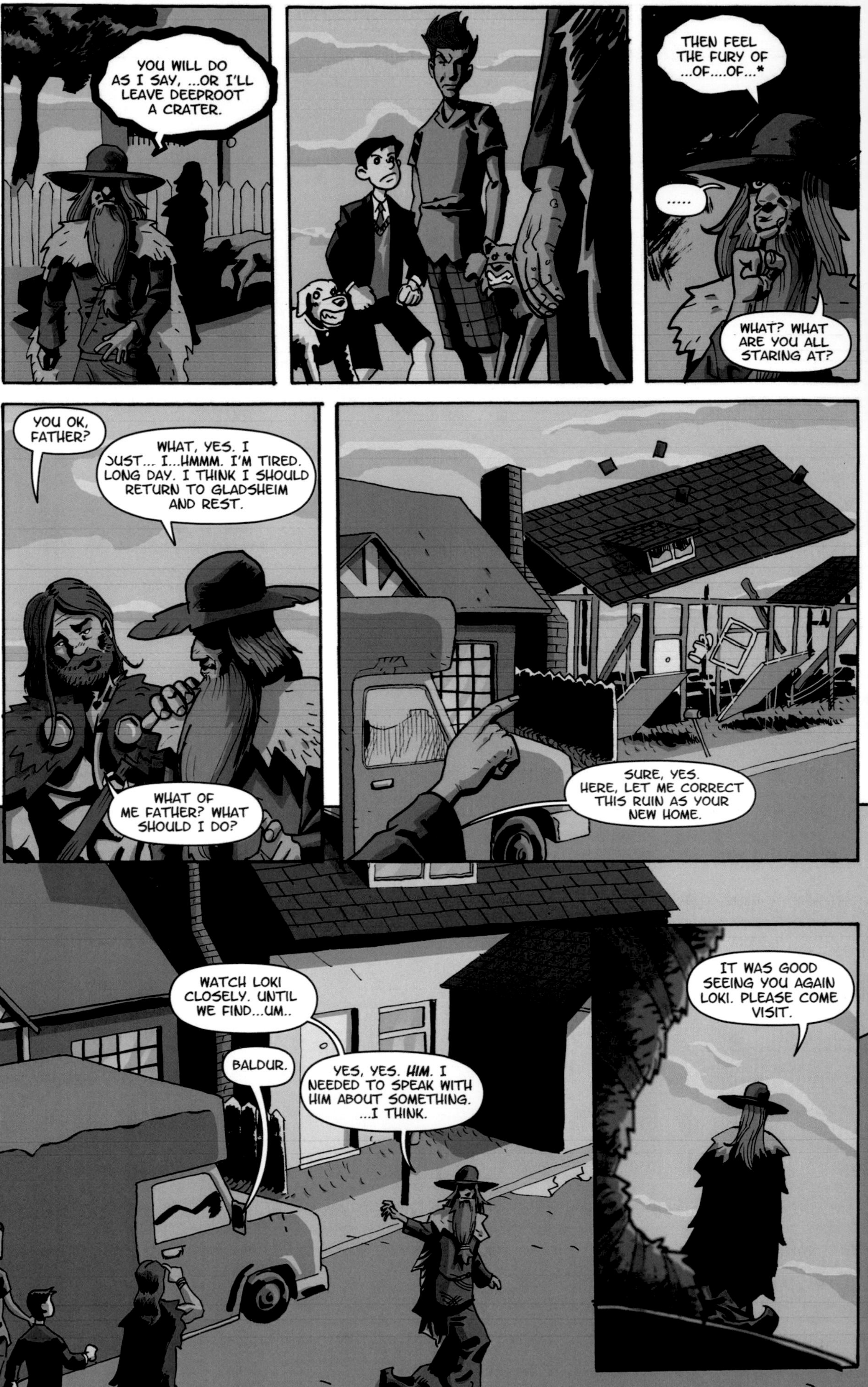
YOU WILL DO AS I SAY, ...OR I'LL LEAVE DEEPROOT A CRATER.
THEN FEEL THE FURY OF ...OF....OF...*
.....
WHAT? WHAT ARE YOU ALL STARING AT?
YOU OK, FATHER?
WHAT, YES. I JUST... I...HMMM. I'M TIRED. LONG DAY. I THINK I SHOULD RETURN TO GLADSHEIM AND REST.
WHAT OF ME FATHER? WHAT SHOULD I DO?
SURE, YES. HERE, LET ME CORRECT THIS RUIN AS YOUR NEW HOME.
WATCH LOKI CLOSELY. UNTIL WE FIND...UM..
BALDUR.
YES, YES. HIM. I NEEDED TO SPEAK WITH HIM ABOUT SOMETHING. ...I THINK.
IT WAS GOOD SEEING YOU AGAIN LOKI. PLEASE COME VISIT.

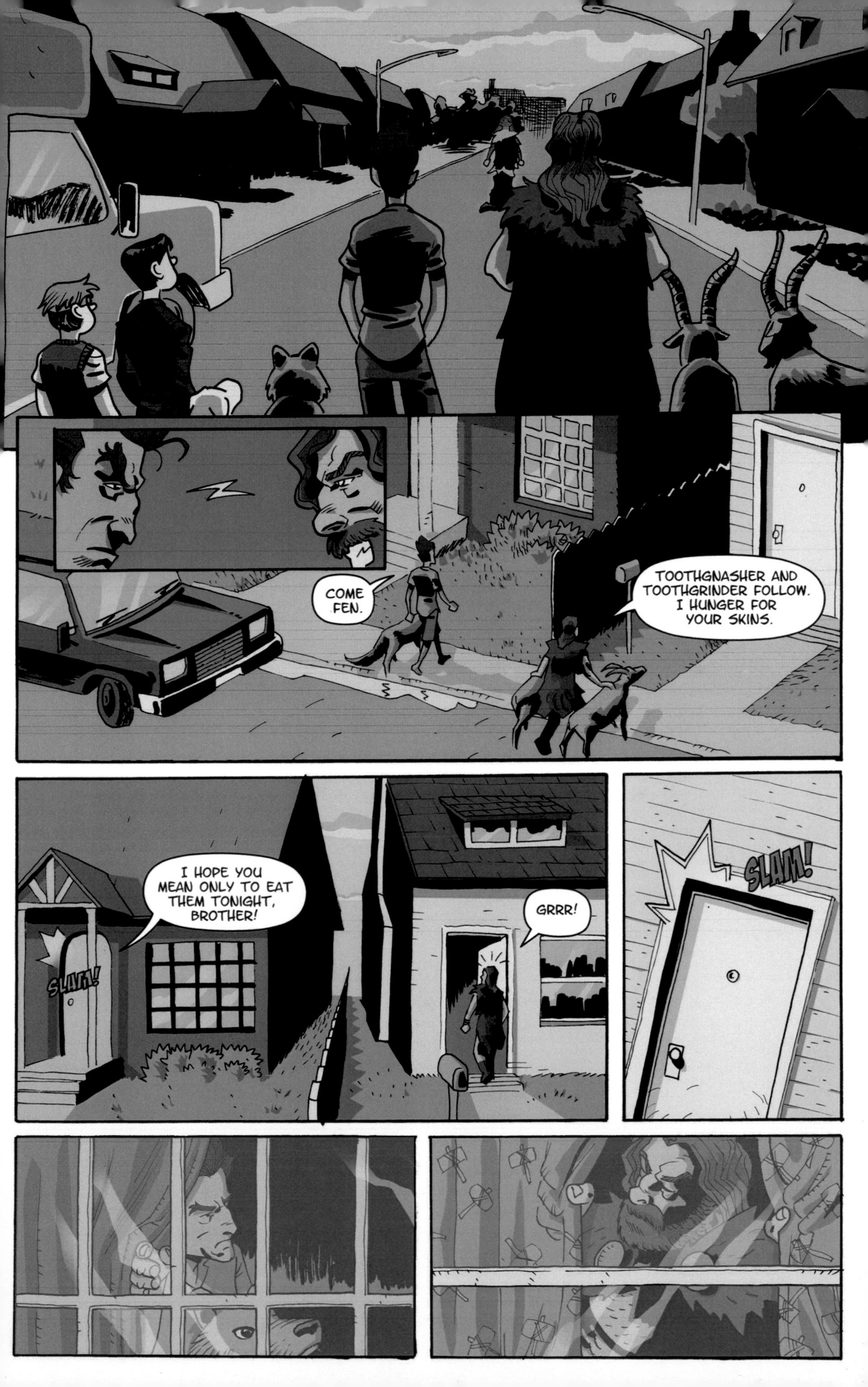
COME FEN.
TOOTHGNASHER AND TOOTHGRINDER FOLLOW. I HUNGER FOR YOUR SKINS.
I HOPE YOU MEAN ONLY TO EAT THEM TONIGHT, BROTHER!
SLAM!
GRRR!
SLAM!

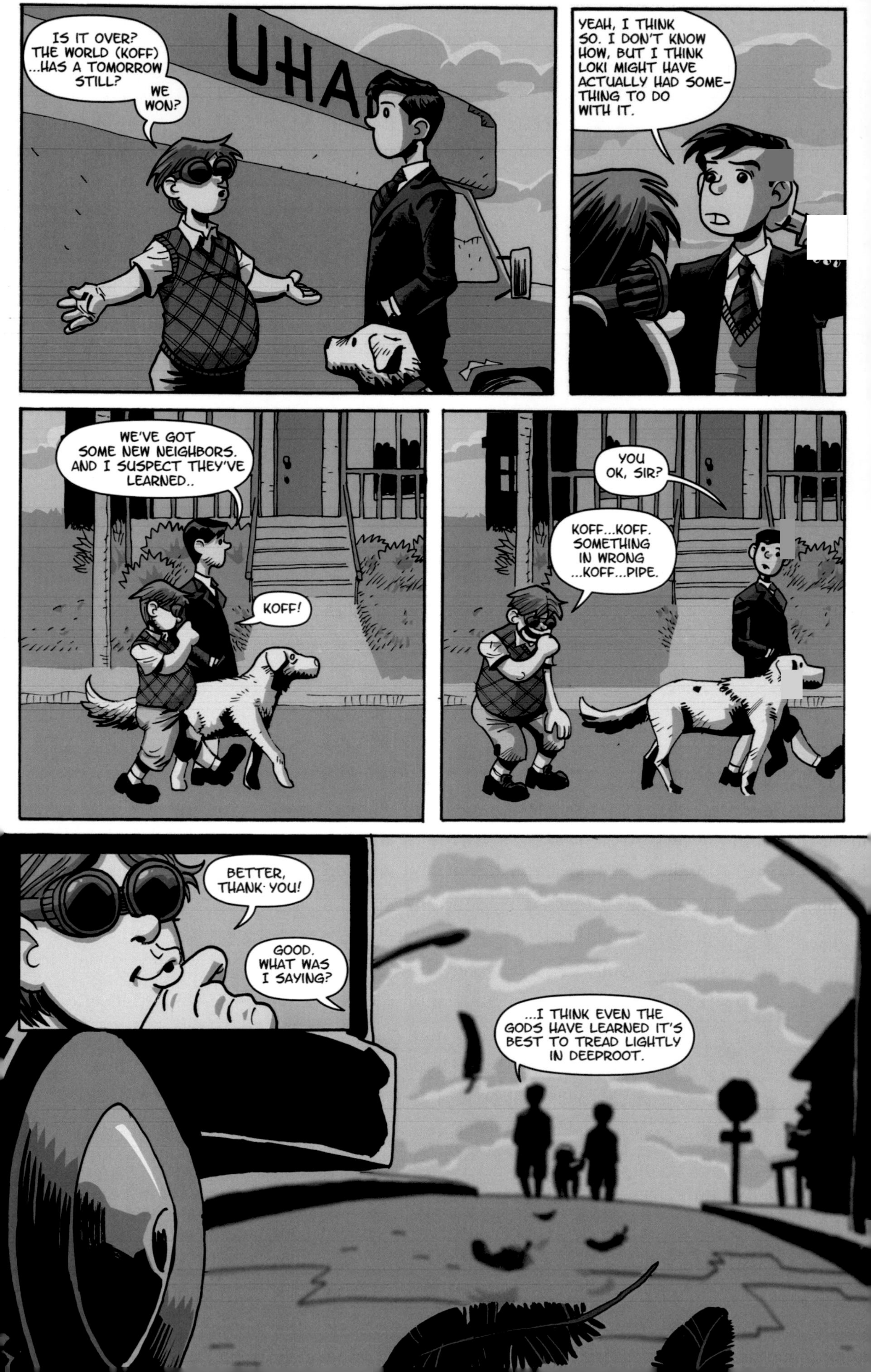
UHA
IS IT OVER? THE WORLD (KOFF) ...HAS A TOMORROW STILL?
WE WON?
YEAH, I THINK SO. I DON'T KNOW HOW, BUT I THINK LOKI MIGHT HAVE ACTUALLY HAD SOME-THING TO DO WITH IT.
WE'VE GOT SOME NEW NEIGHBORS. AND I SUSPECT THEY'VE LEARNED..
KOFF!
YOU OK, SIR?
KOFF...KOFF. SOMETHING IN WRONG ...KOFF...PIPE.
BETTER, THANK YOU!
GOOD. WHAT WAS I SAYING?
...I THINK EVEN THE GODS HAVE LEARNED IT'S BEST TO TREAD LIGHTLY IN DEEPROOT.

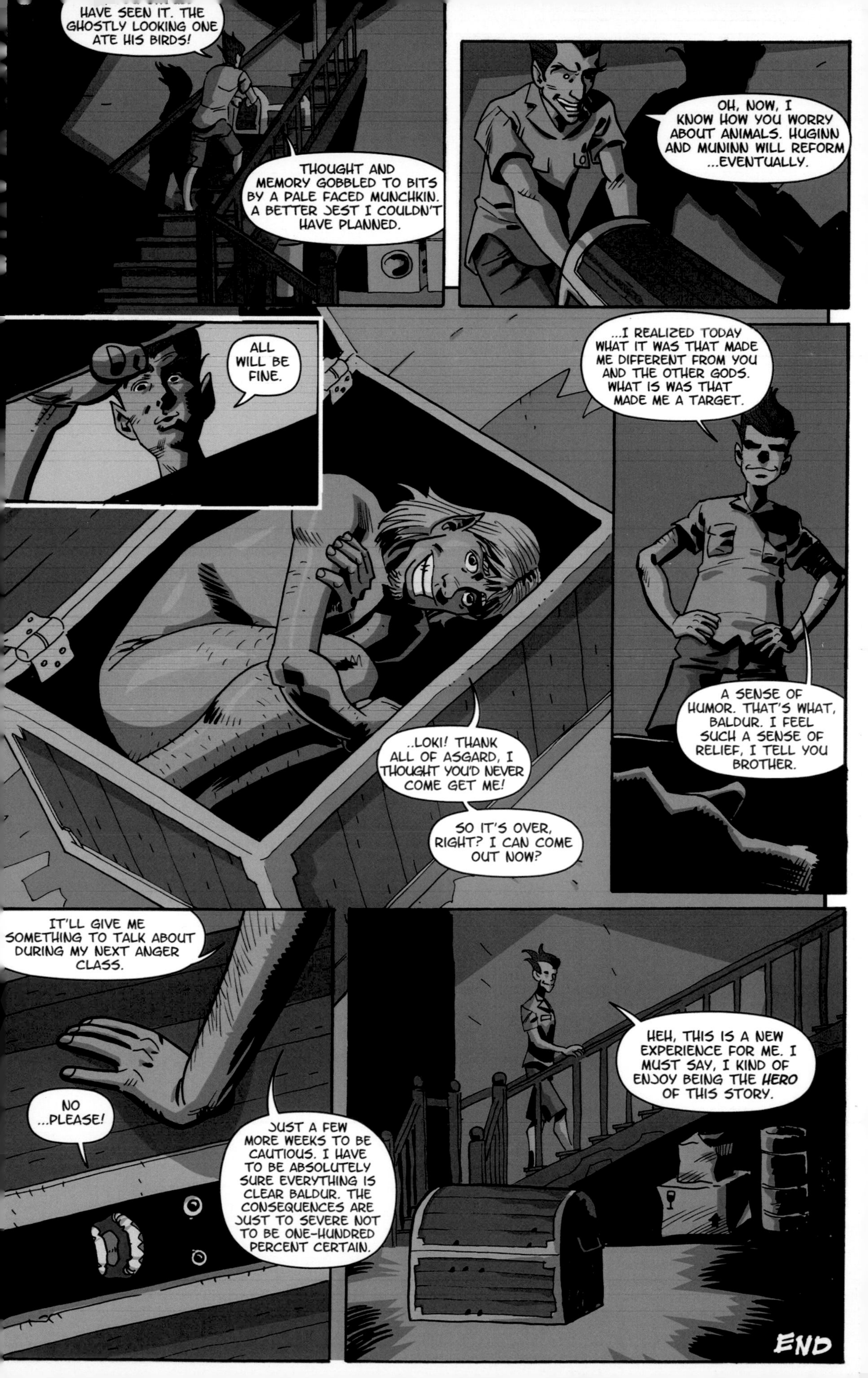
HAVE SEEN IT. THE GHOSTLY LOOKING ONE ATE HIS BIRDS!
THOUGHT AND MEMORY GOBBLED TO BITS BY A PALE FACED MUNCHKIN. A BETTER JEST I COULDN'T HAVE PLANNED.
OH, NOW, I KNOW HOW YOU WORRY ABOUT ANIMALS. HUGINN AND MUNINN WILL REFORM ...EVENTUALLY.
ALL WILL BE FINE.
..LOKI! THANK ALL OF ASGARD, I THOUGHT YOU'D NEVER COME GET ME!
SO IT'S OVER, RIGHT? I CAN COME OUT NOW?
...I REALIZED TODAY WHAT IT WAS THAT MADE ME DIFFERENT FROM YOU AND THE OTHER GODS. WHAT IS WAS THAT MADE ME A TARGET.
A SENSE OF HUMOR. THAT'S WHAT, BALDUR. I FEEL SUCH A SENSE OF RELIEF, I TELL YOU BROTHER.
IT'LL GIVE ME SOMETHING TO TALK ABOUT DURING MY NEXT ANGER CLASS.
NO ...PLEASE!
JUST A FEW MORE WEEKS TO BE CAUTIOUS. I HAVE TO BE ABSOLUTELY SURE EVERYTHING IS CLEAR BALDUR. THE CONSEQUENCES ARE JUST TO SEVERE NOT TO BE ONE-HUNDRED PERCENT CERTAIN.
HEH, THIS IS A NEW EXPERIENCE FOR ME. I MUST SAY, I KIND OF ENJOY BEING THE *HERO* OF THIS STORY.
END

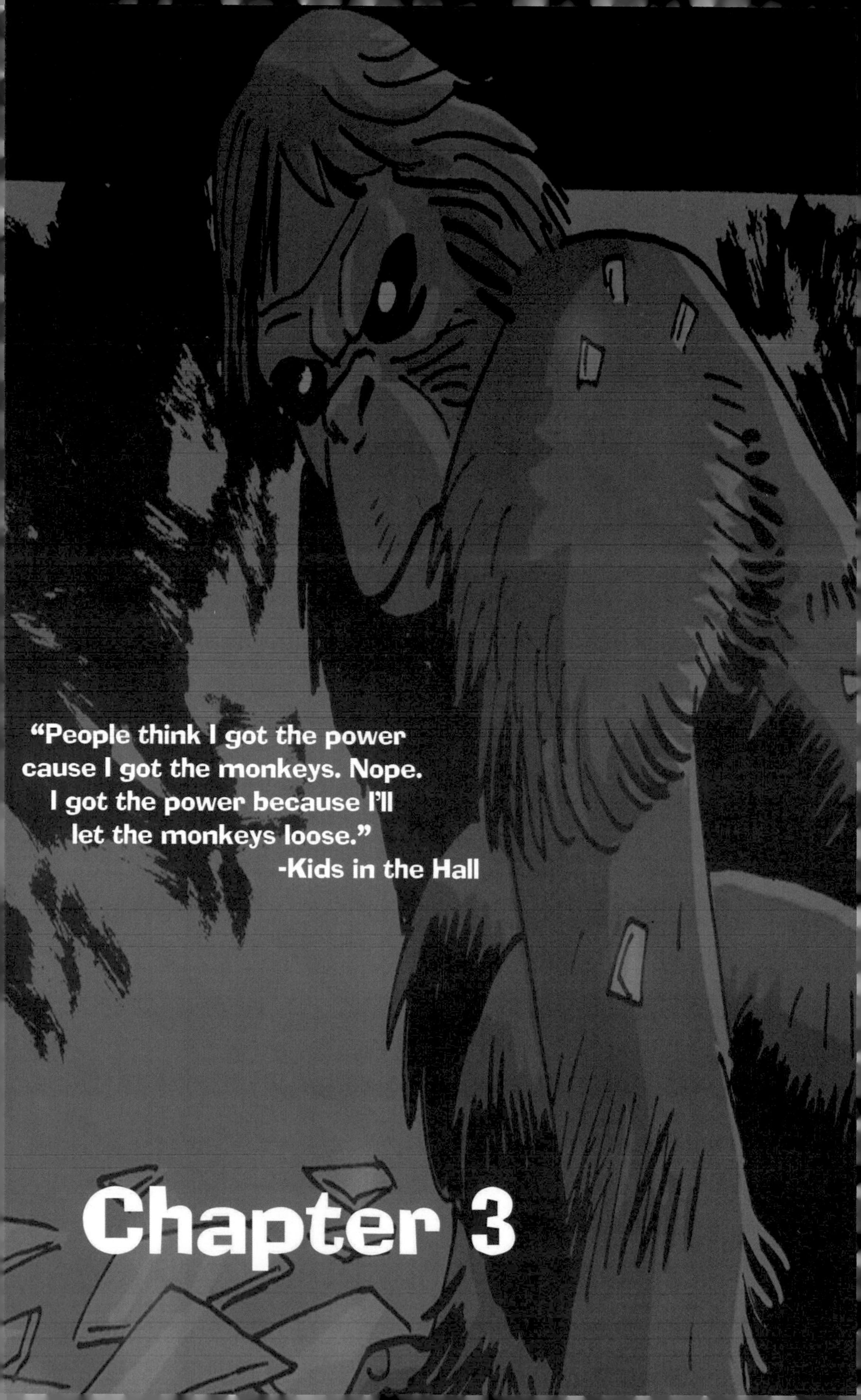

“People think I got the power
cause I got the monkeys. Nope.
I got the power because I’ll
let the monkeys loose.”
-Kids in the Hall

Chapter 3

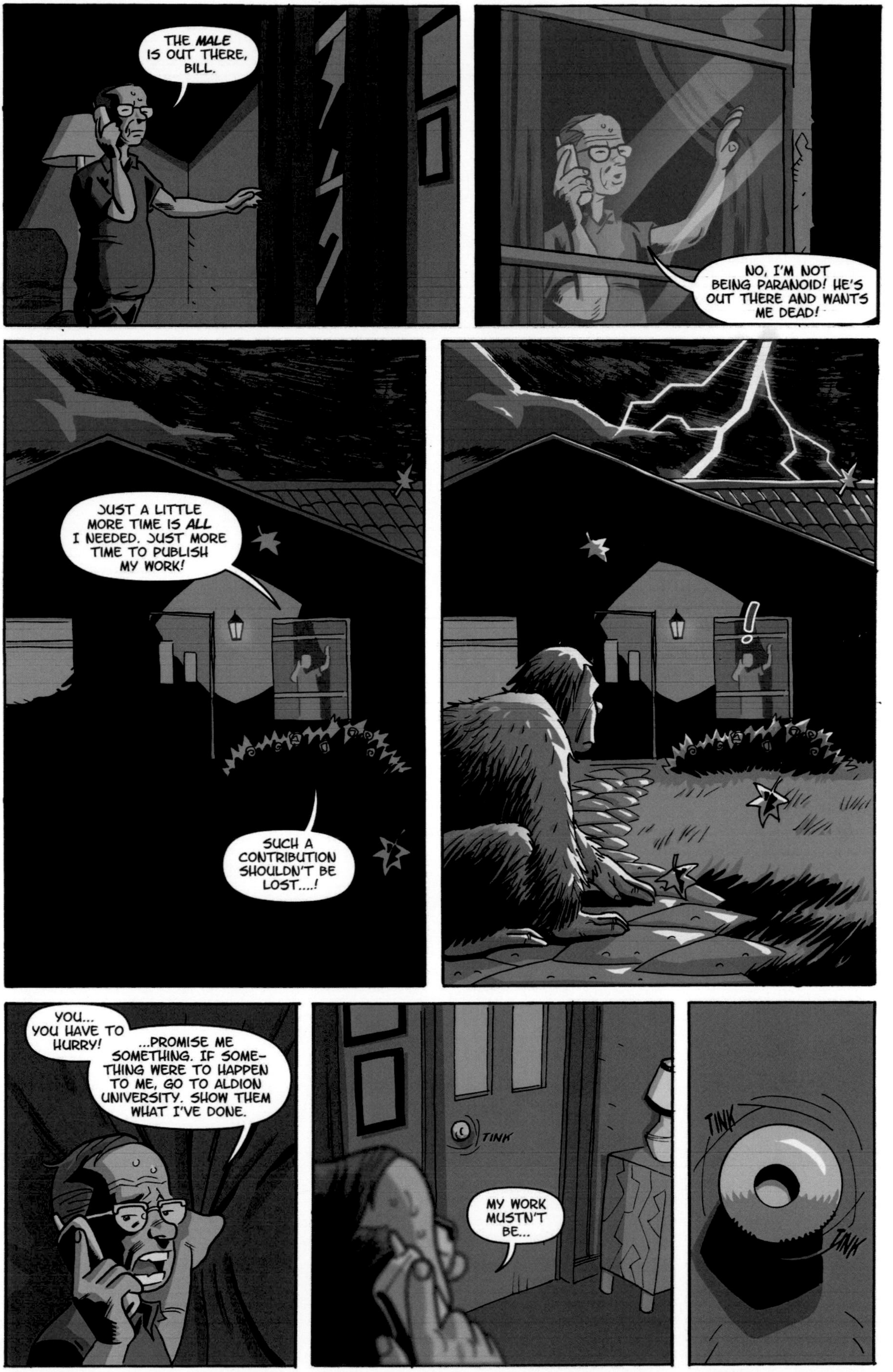

THE MALE IS OUT THERE, BILL.
NO, I'M NOT BEING PARANOID! HE'S OUT THERE AND WANTS ME DEAD!
JUST A LITTLE MORE TIME IS ALL I NEEDED. JUST MORE TIME TO PUBLISH MY WORK!
SUCH A CONTRIBUTION SHOULDN'T BE LOST....!
!
YOU... YOU HAVE TO HURRY!
...PROMISE ME SOMETHING. IF SOMETHING WERE TO HAPPEN TO ME, GO TO ALDION UNIVERSITY. SHOW THEM WHAT I'VE DONE.
TINK
MY WORK MUSTN'T BE...
TINK
TINK

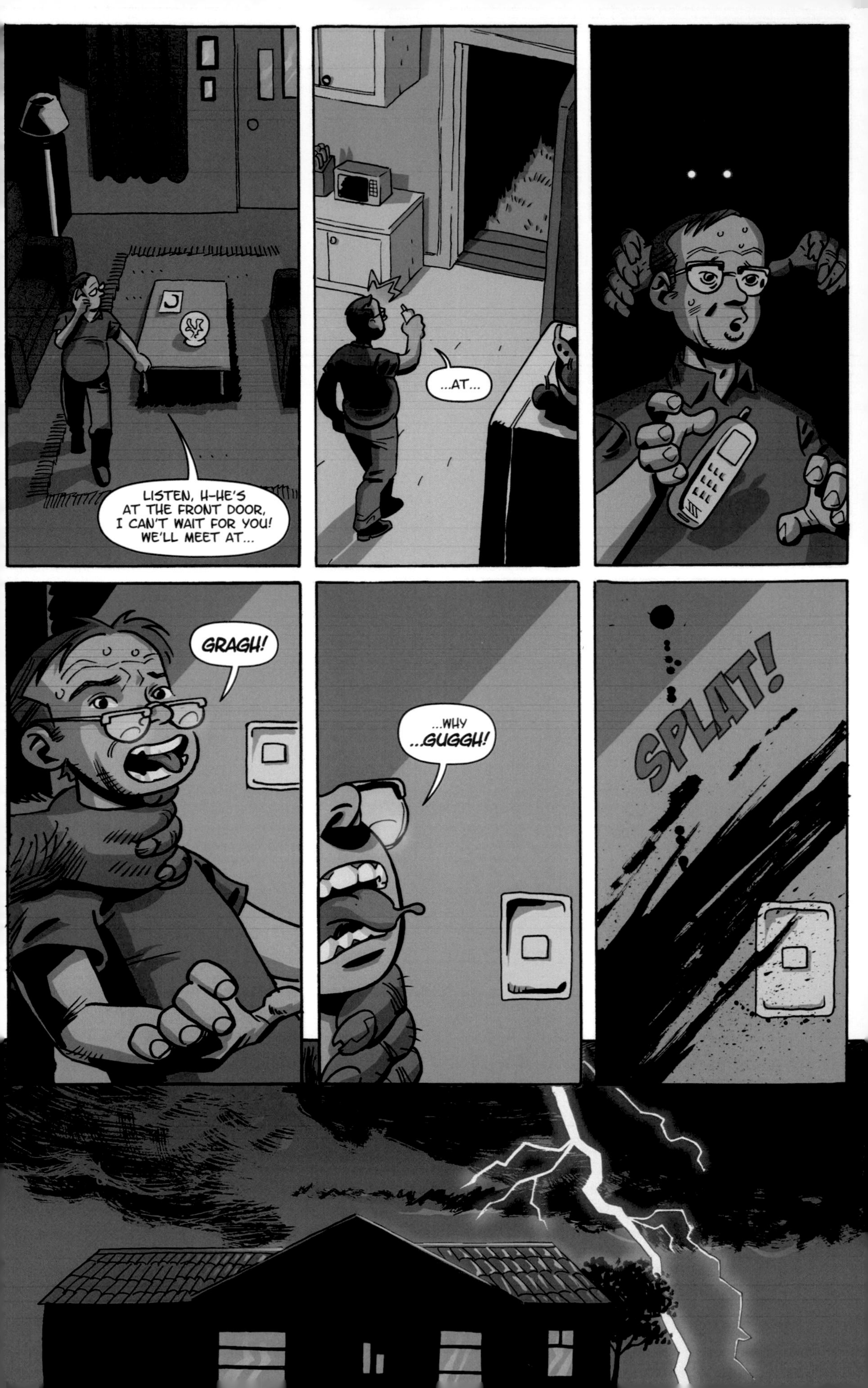
LISTEN, H-HE'S AT THE FRONT DOOR, I CAN'T WAIT FOR YOU! WE'LL MEET AT...
...AT...
GRAGH!
...WHY ...GUGGH!
SPLAT!

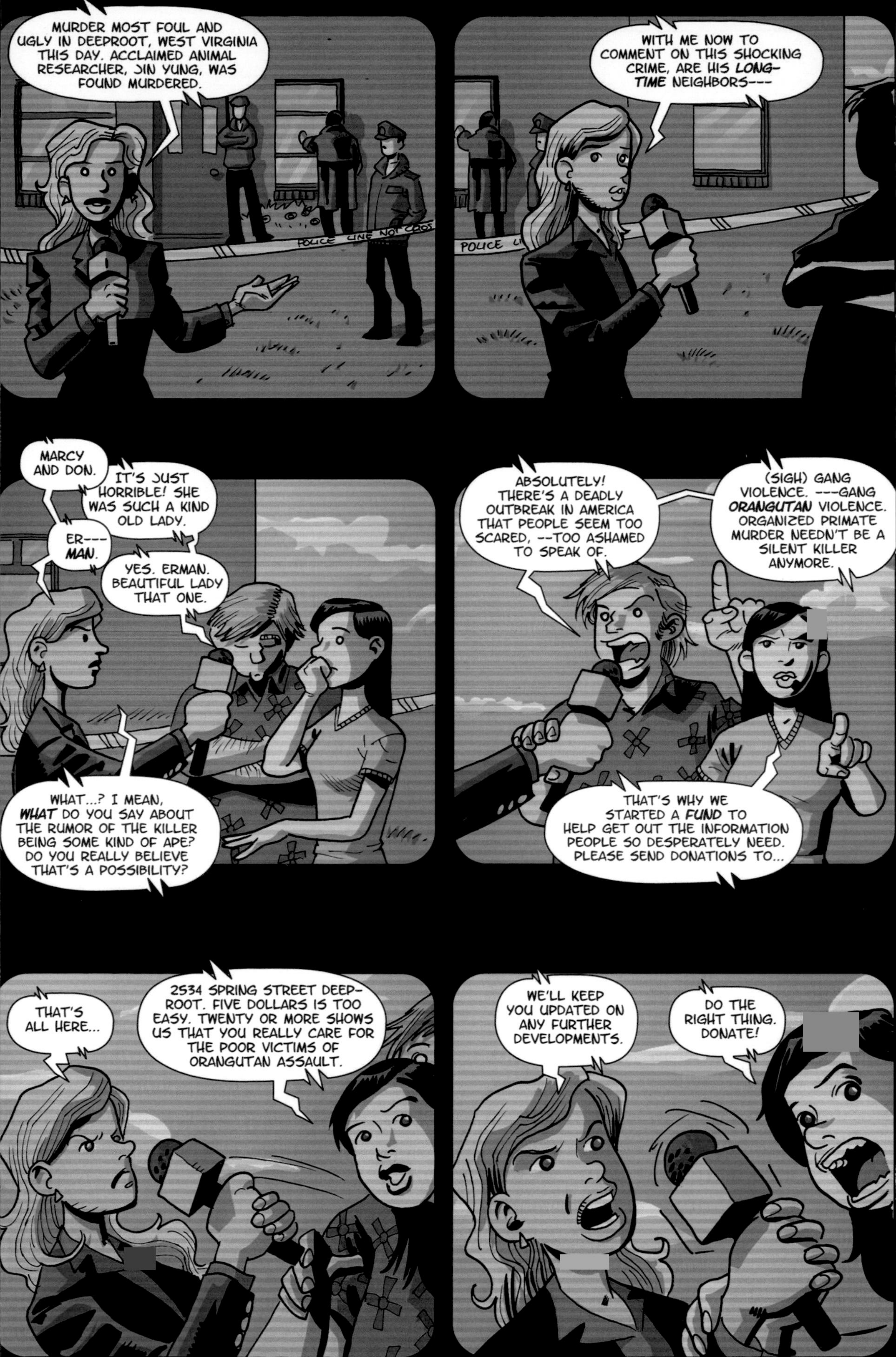
MURDER MOST FOUL AND UGLY IN DEEPROOT, WEST VIRGINIA THIS DAY. ACCLAIMED ANIMAL RESEARCHER, JIN YUNG, WAS FOUND MURDERED.
POLICE LINE NOT CROS
WITH ME NOW TO COMMENT ON THIS SHOCKING CRIME, ARE HIS LONG-TIME NEIGHBORS---
MARCY AND DON.
IT'S JUST HORRIBLE! SHE WAS SUCH A KIND OLD LADY.
ER--- MAN.
YES. ERMAN. BEAUTIFUL LADY THAT ONE.
WHAT...? I MEAN, WHAT DO YOU SAY ABOUT THE RUMOR OF THE KILLER BEING SOME KIND OF APE? DO YOU REALLY BELIEVE THAT'S A POSSIBILITY?
ABSOLUTELY! THERE'S A DEADLY OUTBREAK IN AMERICA THAT PEOPLE SEEM TOO SCARED, --TOO ASHAMED TO SPEAK OF.
(SIGH) GANG VIOLENCE. ---GANG ORANGUTAN VIOLENCE. ORGANIZED PRIMATE MURDER NEEDN'T BE A SILENT KILLER ANYMORE.
THAT'S WHY WE STARTED A FUND TO HELP GET OUT THE INFORMATION PEOPLE SO DESPERATELY NEED. PLEASE SEND DONATIONS TO...
THAT'S ALL HERE...
2534 SPRING STREET DEEP-ROOT. FIVE DOLLARS IS TOO EASY. TWENTY OR MORE SHOWS US THAT YOU REALLY CARE FOR THE POOR VICTIMS OF ORANGUTAN ASSAULT.
WE'LL KEEP YOU UPDATED ON ANY FURTHER DEVELOPMENTS.
DO THE RIGHT THING. DONATE!

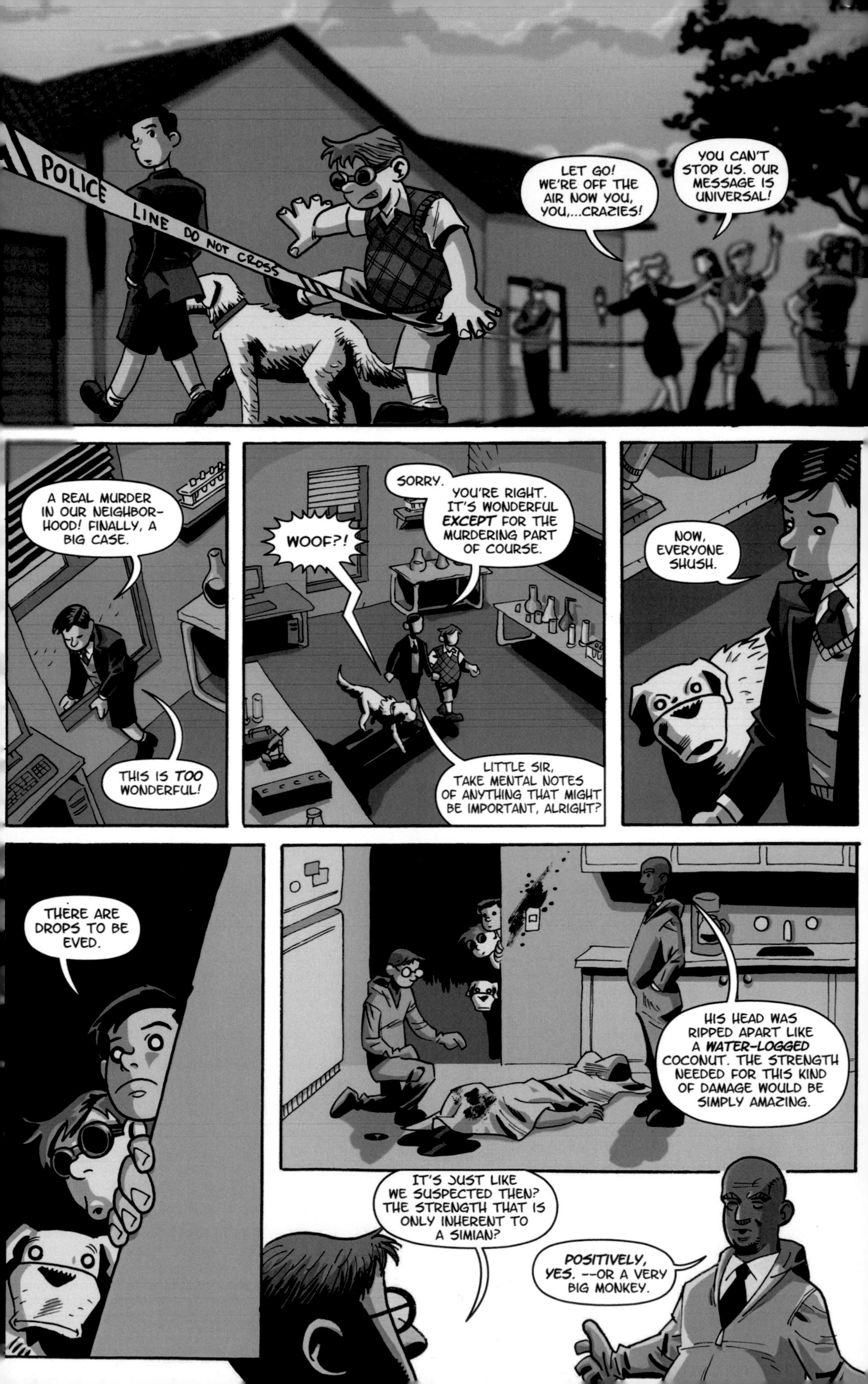
POLICE LINE DO NOT CROSS
LET GO! WE'RE OFF THE AIR NOW YOU, YOU,...CRAZIES!
YOU CAN'T STOP US. OUR MESSAGE IS UNIVERSAL!
A REAL MURDER IN OUR NEIGHBOR-HOOD! FINALLY, A BIG CASE.
THIS IS *TOO* WONDERFUL!
WOOF?!
SORRY.
YOU'RE RIGHT. IT'S WONDERFUL ***EXCEPT*** FOR THE MURDERING PART OF COURSE.
LITTLE SIR, TAKE MENTAL NOTES OF ANYTHING THAT MIGHT BE IMPORTANT, ALRIGHT?
NOW, EVERYONE SHUSH.
THERE ARE DROPS TO BE EYED.
HIS HEAD WAS RIPPED APART LIKE A ***WATER-LOGGED*** COCONUT. THE STRENGTH NEEDED FOR THIS KIND OF DAMAGE WOULD BE SIMPLY AMAZING.
IT'S JUST LIKE WE SUSPECTED THEN? THE STRENGTH THAT IS ONLY INHERENT TO A SIMIAN?
POSITIVELY, YES. --OR A VERY BIG MONKEY.

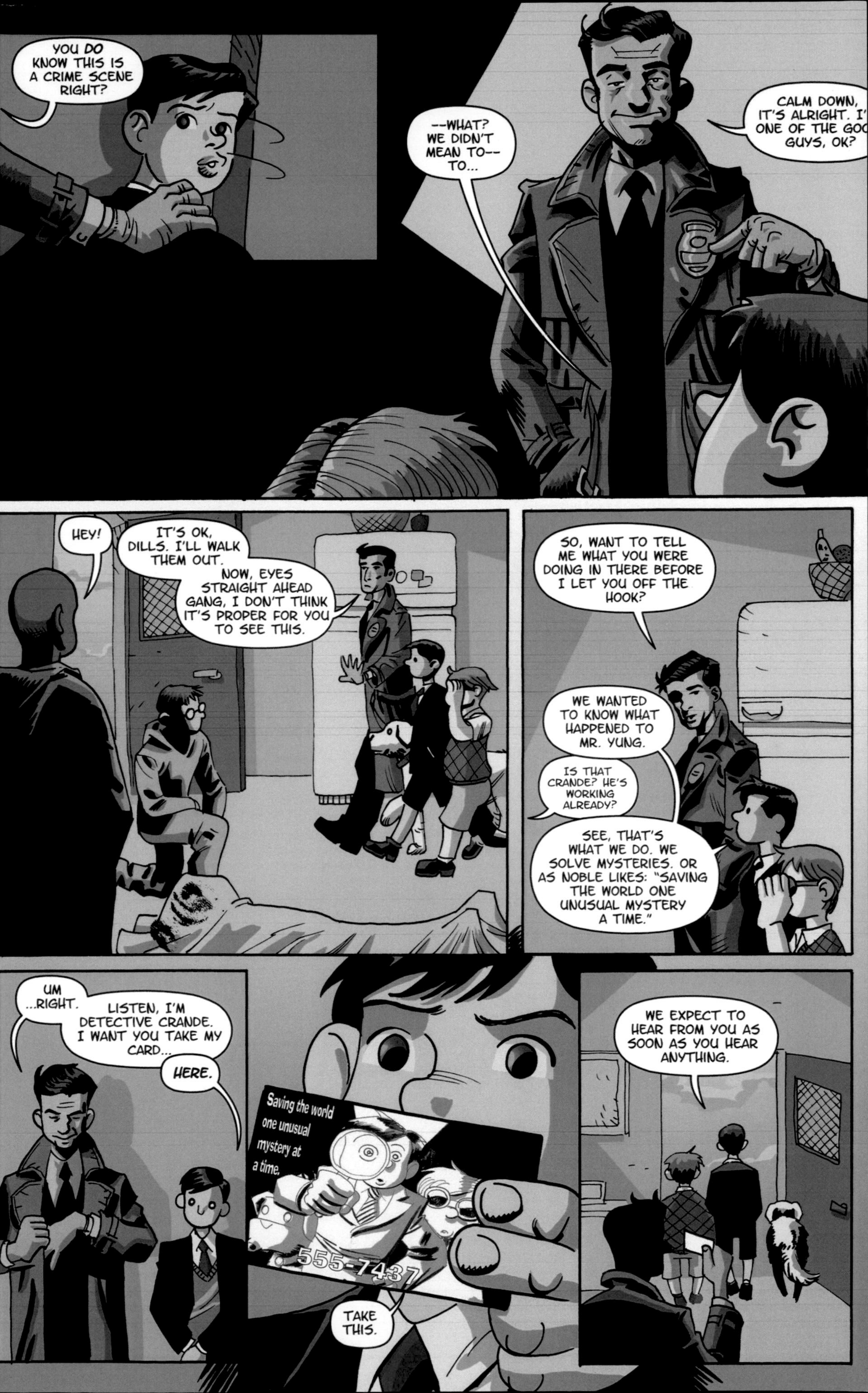
YOU DO KNOW THIS IS A CRIME SCENE RIGHT?
--WHAT? WE DIDN'T MEAN TO--TO...
CALM DOWN, IT'S ALRIGHT. I' ONE OF THE GOO GUYS, OK?
HEY!
IT'S OK, DILLS. I'LL WALK THEM OUT.
NOW, EYES STRAIGHT AHEAD GANG, I DON'T THINK IT'S PROPER FOR YOU TO SEE THIS.
SO, WANT TO TELL ME WHAT YOU WERE DOING IN THERE BEFORE I LET YOU OFF THE HOOK?
WE WANTED TO KNOW WHAT HAPPENED TO MR. YUNG.
IS THAT CRANDE? HE'S WORKING ALREADY?
SEE, THAT'S WHAT WE DO. WE SOLVE MYSTERIES. OR AS NOBLE LIKES: "SAVING THE WORLD ONE UNUSUAL MYSTERY A TIME."
UM ...RIGHT.
LISTEN, I'M DETECTIVE CRANDE. I WANT YOU TAKE MY CARD...
HERE.
Saving the world one unusual mystery at a time.
555-7437
TAKE THIS.
WE EXPECT TO HEAR FROM YOU AS SOON AS YOU HEAR ANYTHING.

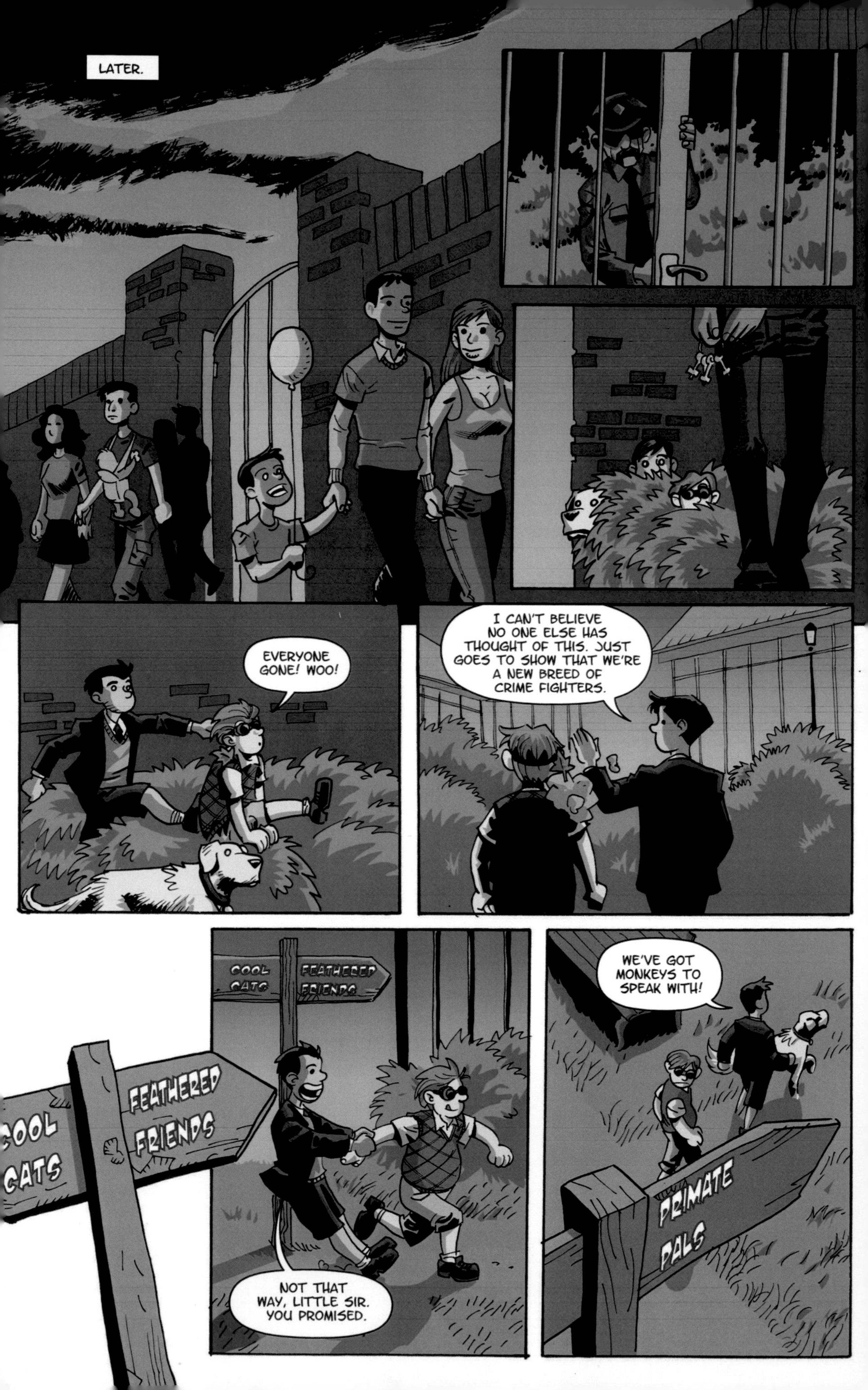
LATER.
EVERYONE GONE! WOO!
I CAN'T BELIEVE NO ONE ELSE HAS THOUGHT OF THIS. JUST GOES TO SHOW THAT WE'RE A NEW BREED OF CRIME FIGHTERS.
COOL CATS
FEATHERED FRIENDS
NOT THAT WAY, LITTLE SIR. YOU PROMISED.
WE'VE GOT MONKEYS TO SPEAK WITH!
PRIMATE PALS

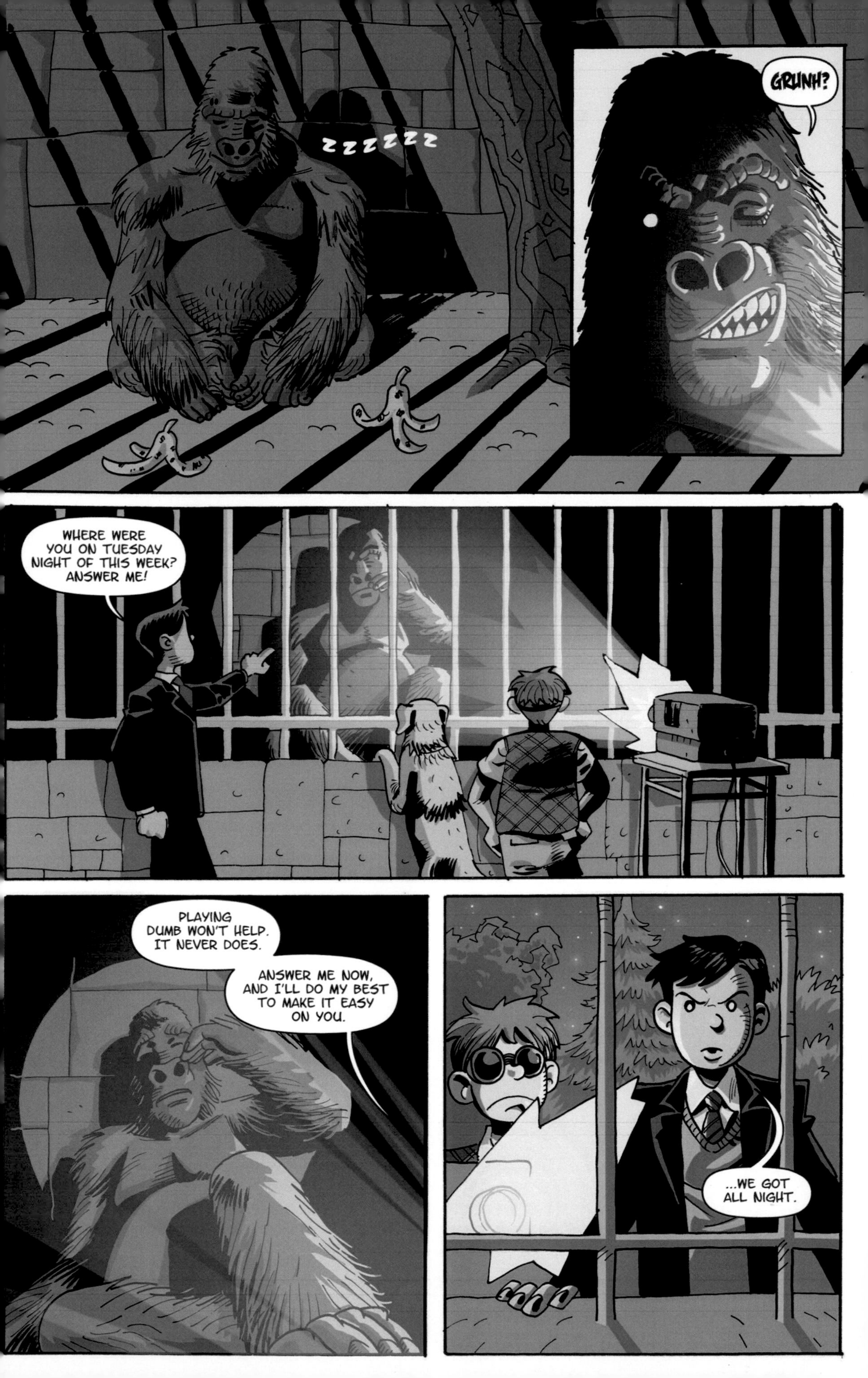
ZZZZZZ
GRUNH?
WHERE WERE YOU ON TUESDAY NIGHT OF THIS WEEK? ANSWER ME!
PLAYING DUMB WON'T HELP. IT NEVER DOES.
ANSWER ME NOW, AND I'LL DO MY BEST TO MAKE IT EASY ON YOU.
...WE GOT ALL NIGHT.

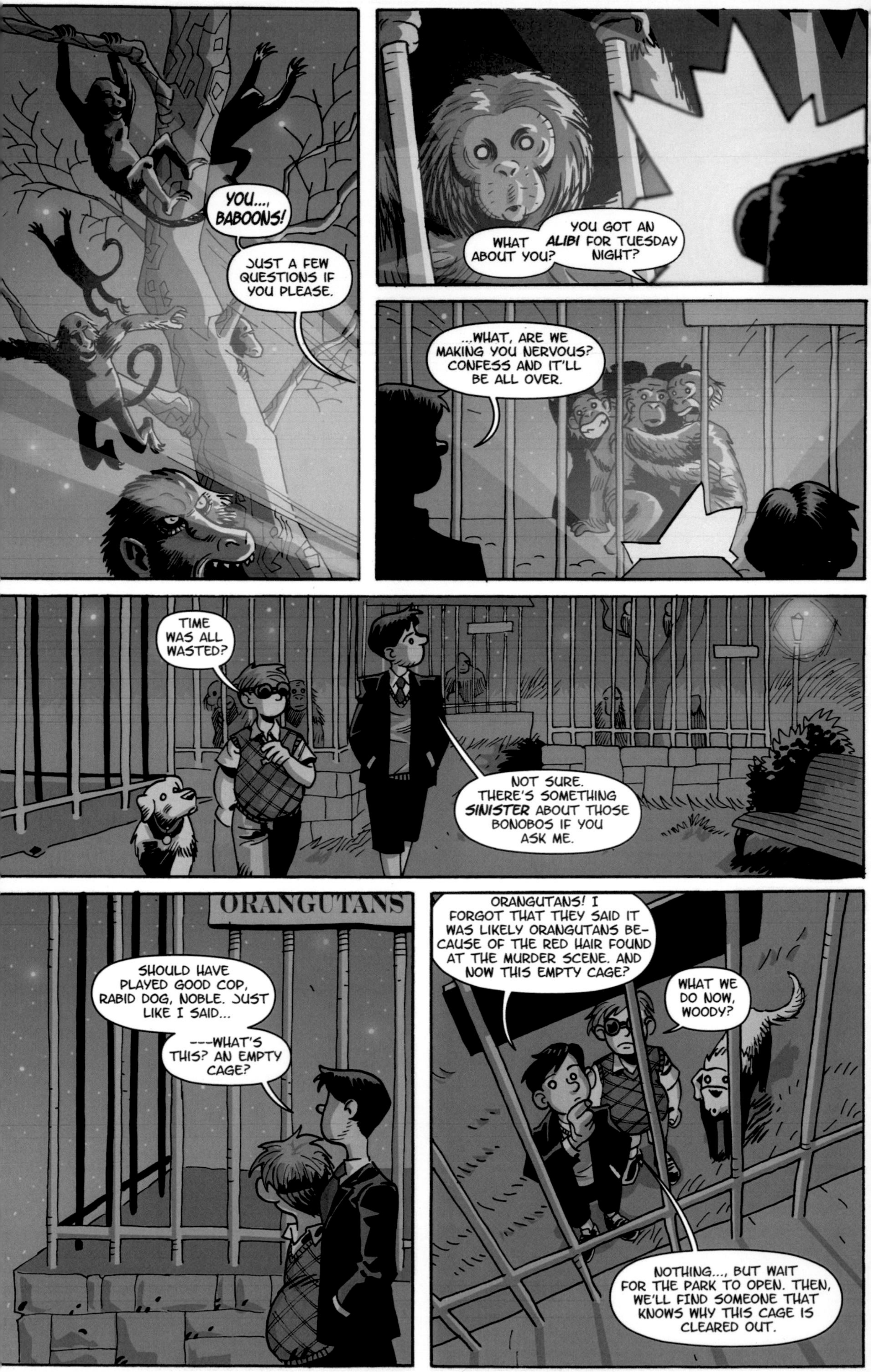
YOU..., BABOONS!
JUST A FEW QUESTIONS IF YOU PLEASE.
WHAT ABOUT YOU?
YOU GOT AN ALIBI FOR TUESDAY NIGHT?
...WHAT, ARE WE MAKING YOU NERVOUS? CONFESS AND IT'LL BE ALL OVER.
TIME WAS ALL WASTED?
NOT SURE. THERE'S SOMETHING SINISTER ABOUT THOSE BONOBOS IF YOU ASK ME.
ORANGUTANS
SHOULD HAVE PLAYED GOOD COP, RABID DOG, NOBLE. JUST LIKE I SAID...
---WHAT'S THIS? AN EMPTY CAGE?
ORANGUTANS! I FORGOT THAT THEY SAID IT WAS LIKELY ORANGUTANS BE-CAUSE OF THE RED HAIR FOUND AT THE MURDER SCENE. AND NOW THIS EMPTY CAGE?
WHAT WE DO NOW, WOODY?
NOTHING..., BUT WAIT FOR THE PARK TO OPEN. THEN, WE'LL FIND SOMEONE THAT KNOWS WHY THIS CAGE IS CLEARED OUT.

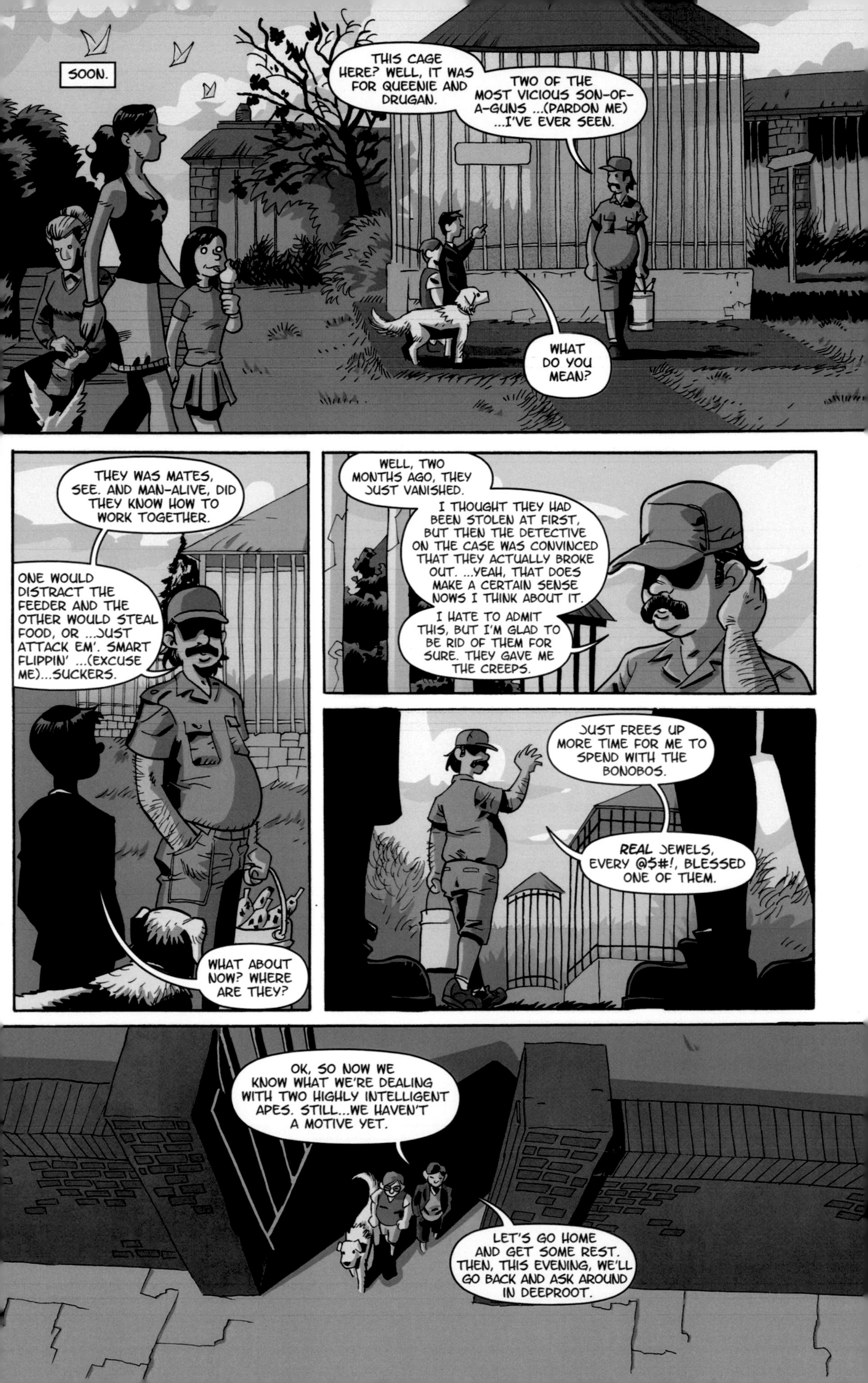
SOON.
THIS CAGE HERE? WELL, IT WAS FOR QUEENIE AND DRUGAN.
TWO OF THE MOST VICIOUS SON-OF-A-GUNS ...(PARDON ME) ...I'VE EVER SEEN.
WHAT DO YOU MEAN?
THEY WAS MATES, SEE. AND MAN-ALIVE, DID THEY KNOW HOW TO WORK TOGETHER.
ONE WOULD DISTRACT THE FEEDER AND THE OTHER WOULD STEAL FOOD, OR ...JUST ATTACK EM'. SMART FLIPPIN' ...(EXCUSE ME)...SUCKERS.
WHAT ABOUT NOW? WHERE ARE THEY?
WELL, TWO MONTHS AGO, THEY JUST VANISHED.
I THOUGHT THEY HAD BEEN STOLEN AT FIRST, BUT THEN THE DETECTIVE ON THE CASE WAS CONVINCED THAT THEY ACTUALLY BROKE OUT. ...YEAH, THAT DOES MAKE A CERTAIN SENSE NOWS I THINK ABOUT IT.
I HATE TO ADMIT THIS, BUT I'M GLAD TO BE RID OF THEM FOR SURE. THEY GAVE ME THE CREEPS.
JUST FREES UP MORE TIME FOR ME TO SPEND WITH THE BONOBOS.
REAL JEWELS, EVERY @$#!, BLESSED ONE OF THEM.
OK, SO NOW WE KNOW WHAT WE'RE DEALING WITH TWO HIGHLY INTELLIGENT APES. STILL...WE HAVEN'T A MOTIVE YET.
LET'S GO HOME AND GET SOME REST. THEN, THIS EVENING, WE'LL GO BACK AND ASK AROUND IN DEEPROOT.

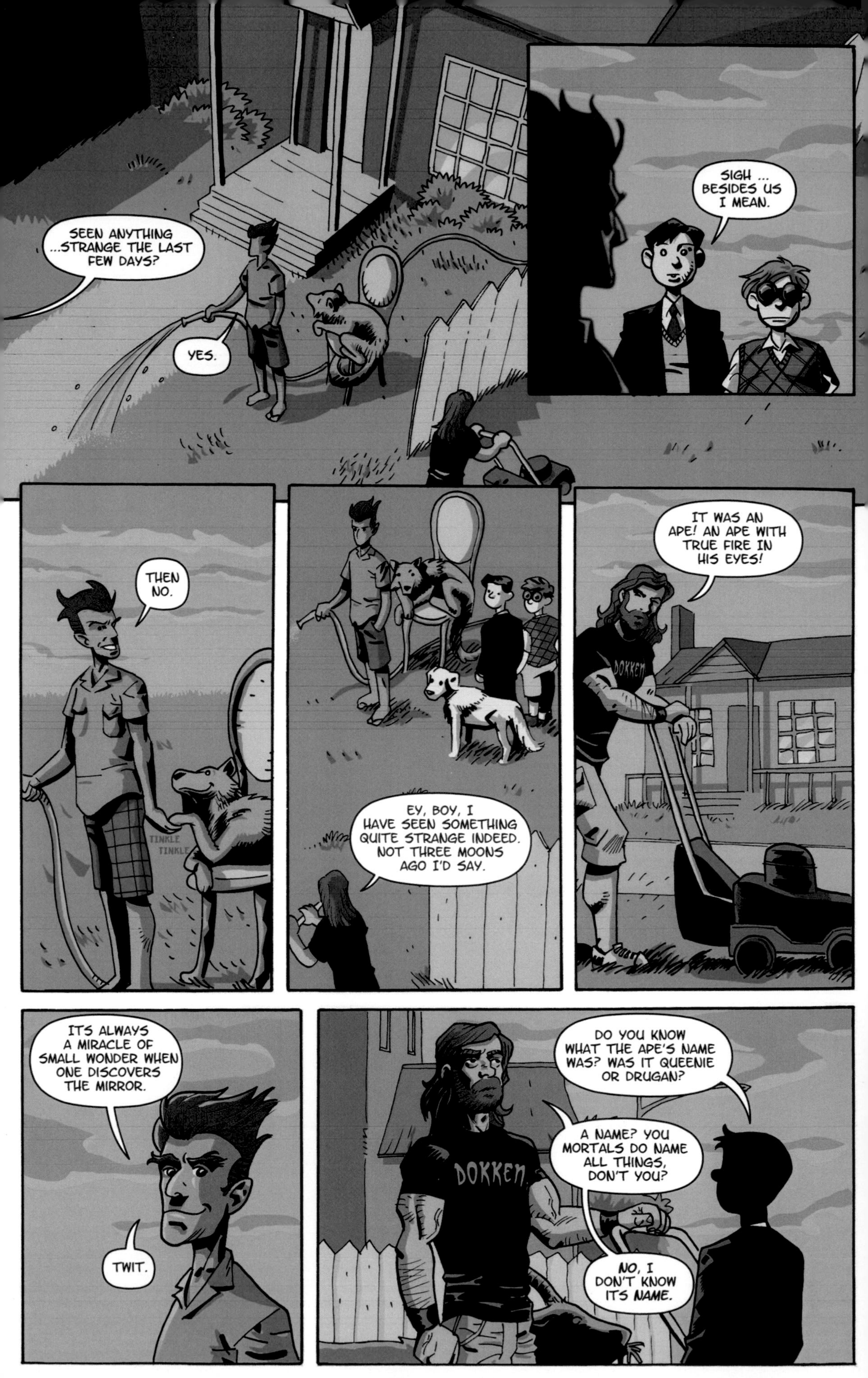
SEEN ANYTHING ...STRANGE THE LAST FEW DAYS?
YES.
SIGH ... BESIDES US I MEAN.
THEN NO.
TINKLE TINKLE
EY, BOY, I HAVE SEEN SOMETHING QUITE STRANGE INDEED. NOT THREE MOONS AGO I'D SAY.
IT WAS AN APE! AN APE WITH TRUE FIRE IN HIS EYES!
DOKKEN
ITS ALWAYS A MIRACLE OF SMALL WONDER WHEN ONE DISCOVERS THE MIRROR.
TWIT.
DO YOU KNOW WHAT THE APE'S NAME WAS? WAS IT QUEENIE OR DRUGAN?
A NAME? YOU MORTALS DO NAME ALL THINGS, DON'T YOU?
NO, I DON'T KNOW ITS NAME.
DOKKEN

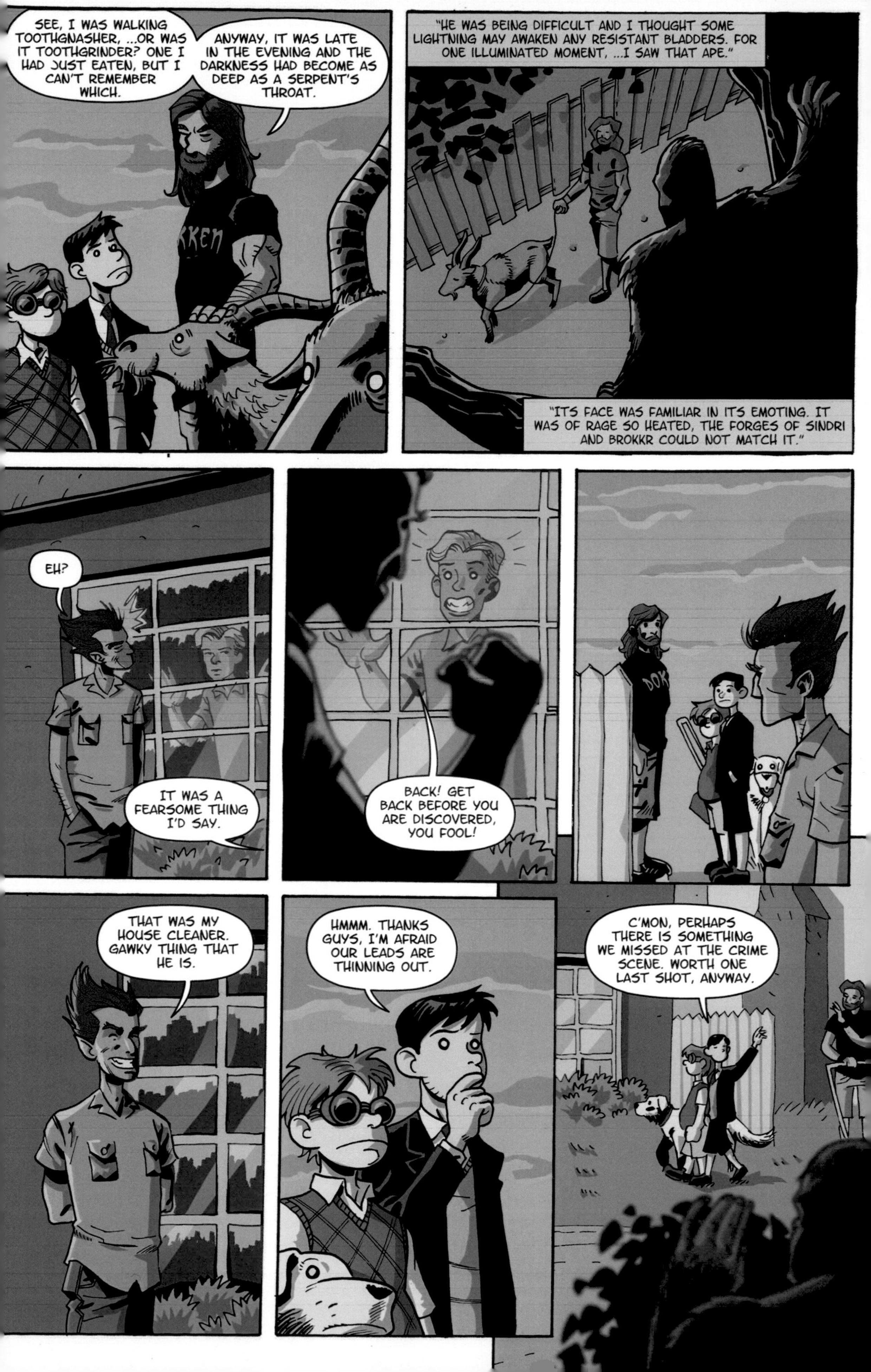
SEE, I WAS WALKING TOOTHGNASHER, ...OR WAS IT TOOTHGRINDER? ONE I HAD JUST EATEN, BUT I CAN'T REMEMBER WHICH.
ANYWAY, IT WAS LATE IN THE EVENING AND THE DARKNESS HAD BECOME AS DEEP AS A SERPENT'S THROAT.
"HE WAS BEING DIFFICULT AND I THOUGHT SOME LIGHTNING MAY AWAKEN ANY RESISTANT BLADDERS. FOR ONE ILLUMINATED MOMENT, ...I SAW THAT APE."
"ITS FACE WAS FAMILIAR IN ITS EMOTING. IT WAS OF RAGE SO HEATED, THE FORGES OF SINDRI AND BROKKR COULD NOT MATCH IT."
EH?
IT WAS A FEARSOME THING I'D SAY.
BACK! GET BACK BEFORE YOU ARE DISCOVERED, YOU FOOL!
THAT WAS MY HOUSE CLEANER. GAWKY THING THAT HE IS.
HMMM. THANKS GUYS, I'M AFRAID OUR LEADS ARE THINNING OUT.
C'MON, PERHAPS THERE IS SOMETHING WE MISSED AT THE CRIME SCENE. WORTH ONE LAST SHOT, ANYWAY.

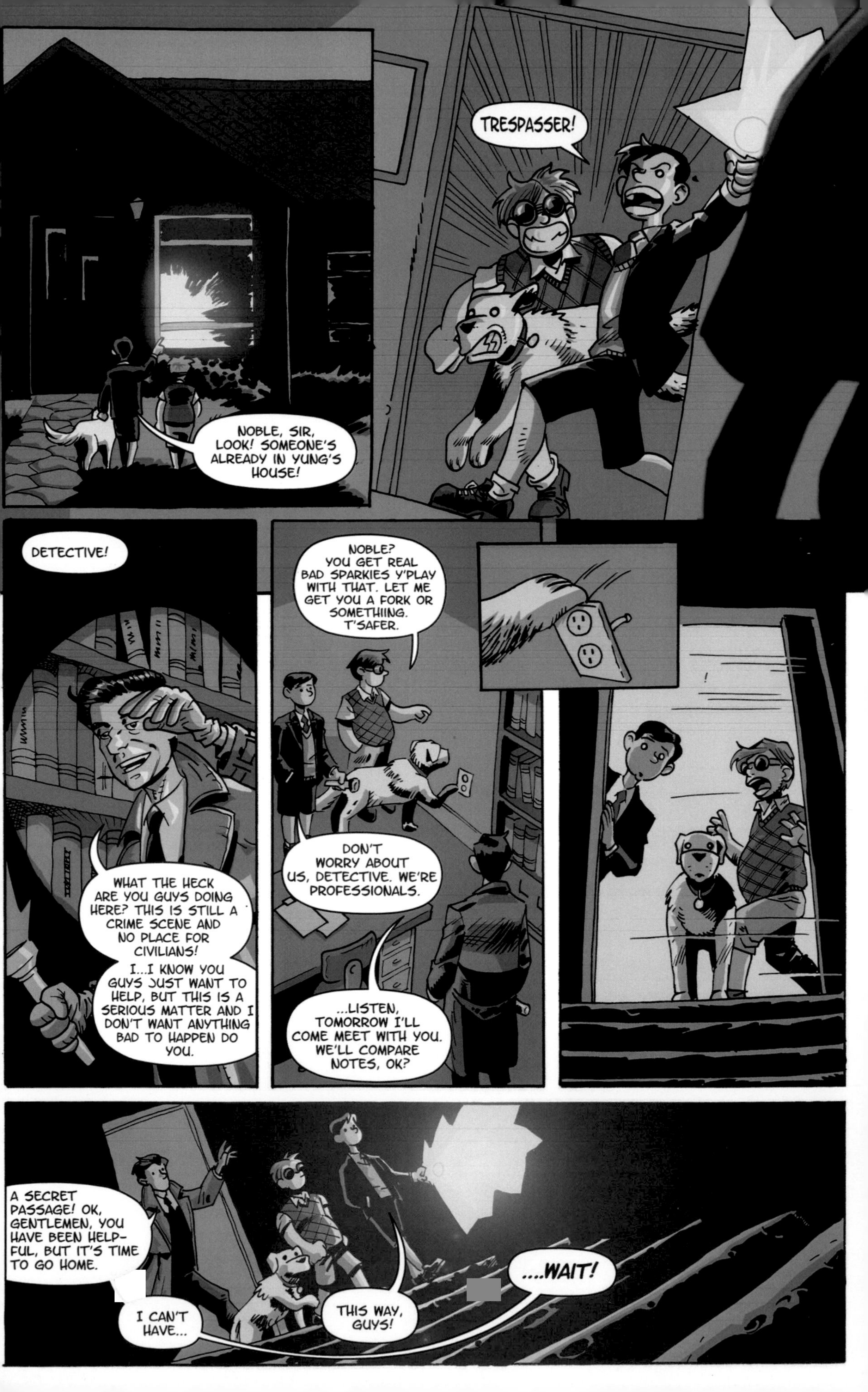
NOBLE, SIR, LOOK! SOMEONE'S ALREADY IN YUNG'S HOUSE!
TRESPASSER!
DETECTIVE!
WHAT THE HECK ARE YOU GUYS DOING HERE? THIS IS STILL A CRIME SCENE AND NO PLACE FOR CIVILIANS!
I...I KNOW YOU GUYS JUST WANT TO HELP, BUT THIS IS A SERIOUS MATTER AND I DON'T WANT ANYTHING BAD TO HAPPEN DO YOU.
NOBLE? YOU GET REAL BAD SPARKIES Y'PLAY WITH THAT. LET ME GET YOU A FORK OR SOMETHIING. T'SAFER.
DON'T WORRY ABOUT US, DETECTIVE. WE'RE PROFESSIONALS.
...LISTEN, TOMORROW I'LL COME MEET WITH YOU. WE'LL COMPARE NOTES, OK?
!
A SECRET PASSAGE! OK, GENTLEMEN, YOU HAVE BEEN HELP-FUL, BUT IT'S TIME TO GO HOME.
I CAN'T HAVE...
THIS WAY, GUYS!
....WAIT!

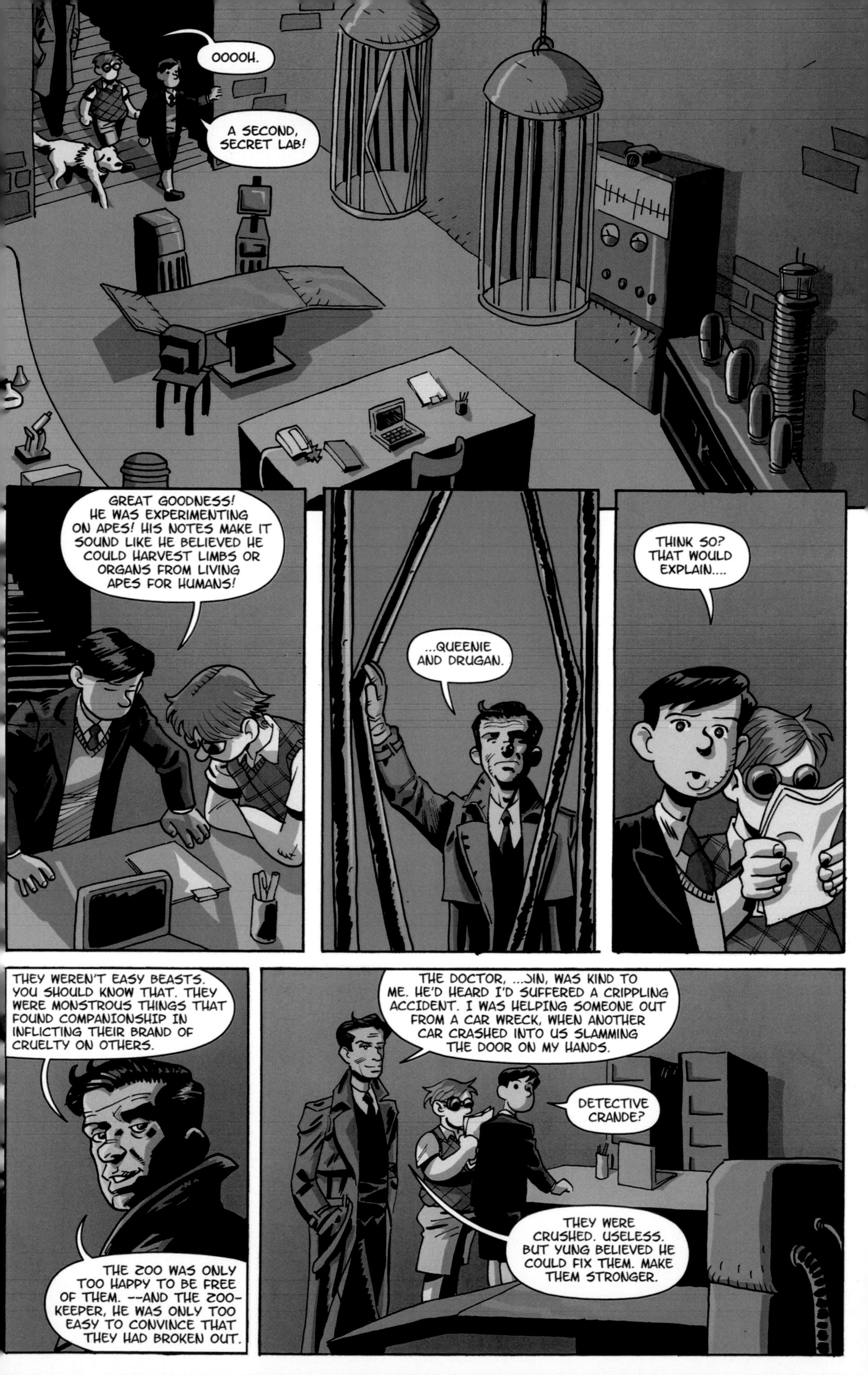
OOOOH.
A SECOND, SECRET LAB!
GREAT GOODNESS! HE WAS EXPERIMENTING ON APES! HIS NOTES MAKE IT SOUND LIKE HE BELIEVED HE COULD HARVEST LIMBS OR ORGANS FROM LIVING APES FOR HUMANS!
...QUEENIE AND DRUGAN.
THINK SO? THAT WOULD EXPLAIN....
THEY WEREN'T EASY BEASTS. YOU SHOULD KNOW THAT. THEY WERE MONSTROUS THINGS THAT FOUND COMPANIONSHIP IN INFLICTING THEIR BRAND OF CRUELTY ON OTHERS.
THE ZOO WAS ONLY TOO HAPPY TO BE FREE OF THEM. --AND THE ZOO-KEEPER, HE WAS ONLY TOO EASY TO CONVINCE THAT THEY HAD BROKEN OUT.
THE DOCTOR, ...JIN, WAS KIND TO ME. HE'D HEARD I'D SUFFERED A CRIPPLING ACCIDENT. I WAS HELPING SOMEONE OUT FROM A CAR WRECK, WHEN ANOTHER CAR CRASHED INTO US SLAMMING THE DOOR ON MY HANDS.
DETECTIVE CRANDE?
THEY WERE CRUSHED. USELESS. BUT YUNG BELIEVED HE COULD FIX THEM. MAKE THEM STRONGER.

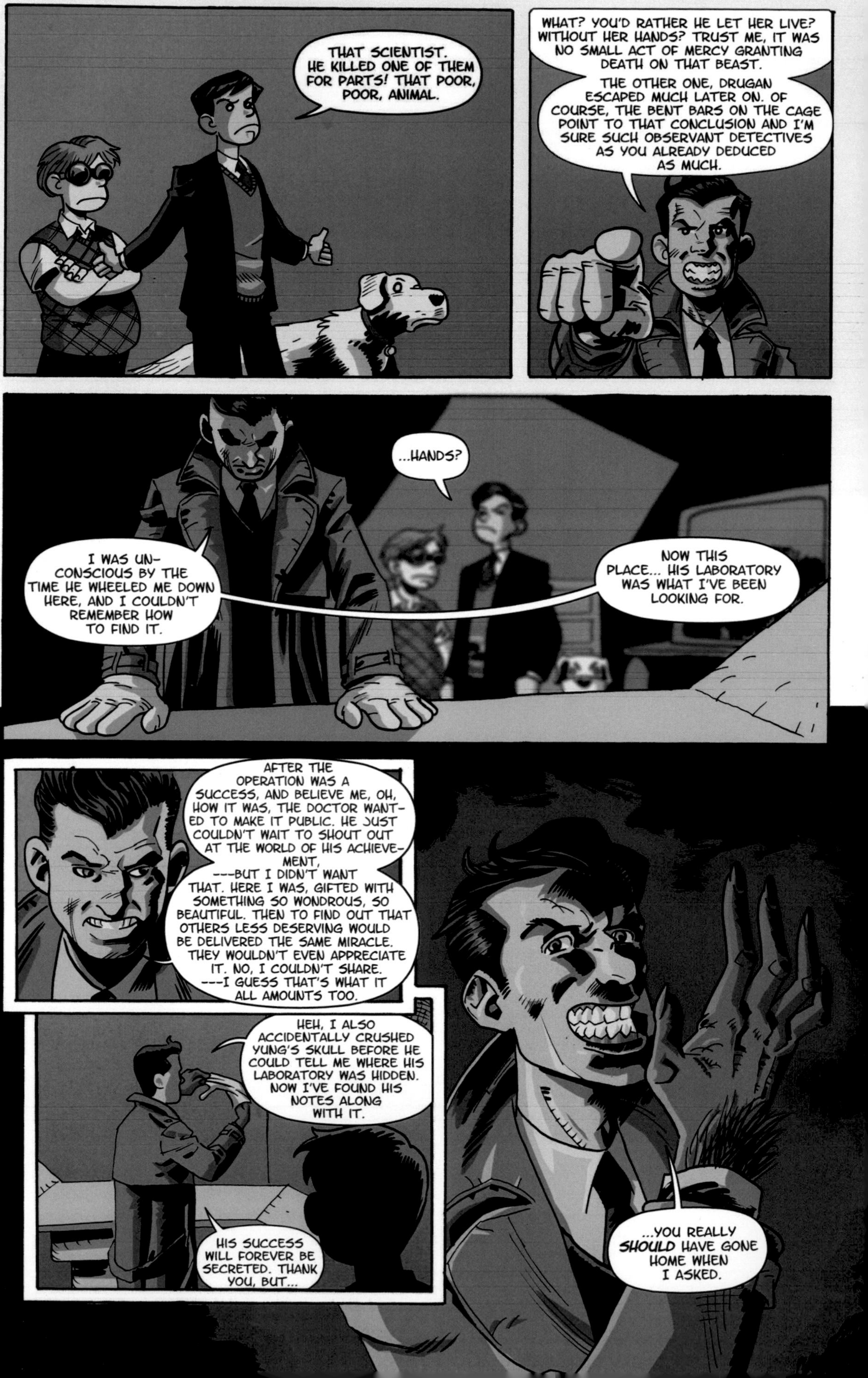
THAT SCIENTIST. HE KILLED ONE OF THEM FOR PARTS! THAT POOR, POOR, ANIMAL.
WHAT? YOU'D RATHER HE LET HER LIVE? WITHOUT HER HANDS? TRUST ME, IT WAS NO SMALL ACT OF MERCY GRANTING DEATH ON THAT BEAST.
THE OTHER ONE, DRUGAN ESCAPED MUCH LATER ON. OF COURSE, THE BENT BARS ON THE CAGE POINT TO THAT CONCLUSION AND I'M SURE SUCH OBSERVANT DETECTIVES AS YOU ALREADY DEDUCED AS MUCH.
...HANDS?
I WAS UN-CONSCIOUS BY THE TIME HE WHEELED ME DOWN HERE, AND I COULDN'T REMEMBER HOW TO FIND IT.
NOW THIS PLACE... HIS LABORATORY WAS WHAT I'VE BEEN LOOKING FOR.
AFTER THE OPERATION WAS A SUCCESS, AND BELIEVE ME, OH, HOW IT WAS, THE DOCTOR WANT-ED TO MAKE IT PUBLIC. HE JUST COULDN'T WAIT TO SHOUT OUT AT THE WORLD OF HIS ACHIEVE-MENT,
---BUT I DIDN'T WANT THAT. HERE I WAS, GIFTED WITH SOMETHING SO WONDROUS, SO BEAUTIFUL. THEN TO FIND OUT THAT OTHERS LESS DESERVING WOULD BE DELIVERED THE SAME MIRACLE. THEY WOULDN'T EVEN APPRECIATE IT. NO, I COULDN'T SHARE. ---I GUESS THAT'S WHAT IT ALL AMOUNTS TOO.
HEH, I ALSO ACCIDENTALLY CRUSHED YUNG'S SKULL BEFORE HE COULD TELL ME WHERE HIS LABORATORY WAS HIDDEN. NOW I'VE FOUND HIS NOTES ALONG WITH IT.
HIS SUCCESS WILL FOREVER BE SECRETED. THANK YOU, BUT...
...YOU REALLY **SHOULD** HAVE GONE HOME WHEN I ASKED.

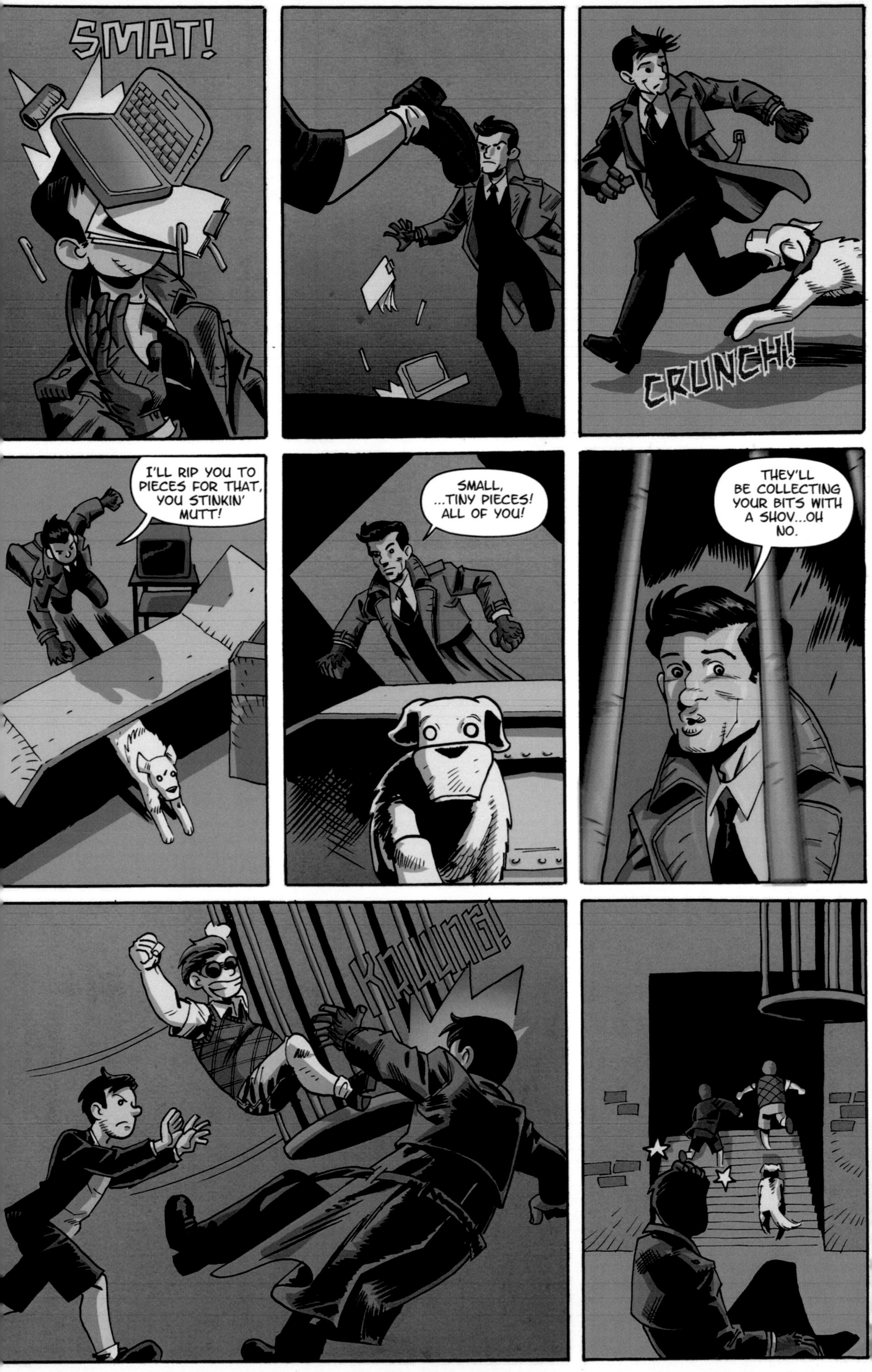
SMAT!
CRUNCH!
I'LL RIP YOU TO PIECES FOR THAT, YOU STINKIN' MUTT!
SMALL, ...TINY PIECES! ALL OF YOU!
THEY'LL BE COLLECTING YOUR BITS WITH A SHOV...OH NO.
KRUUNG!

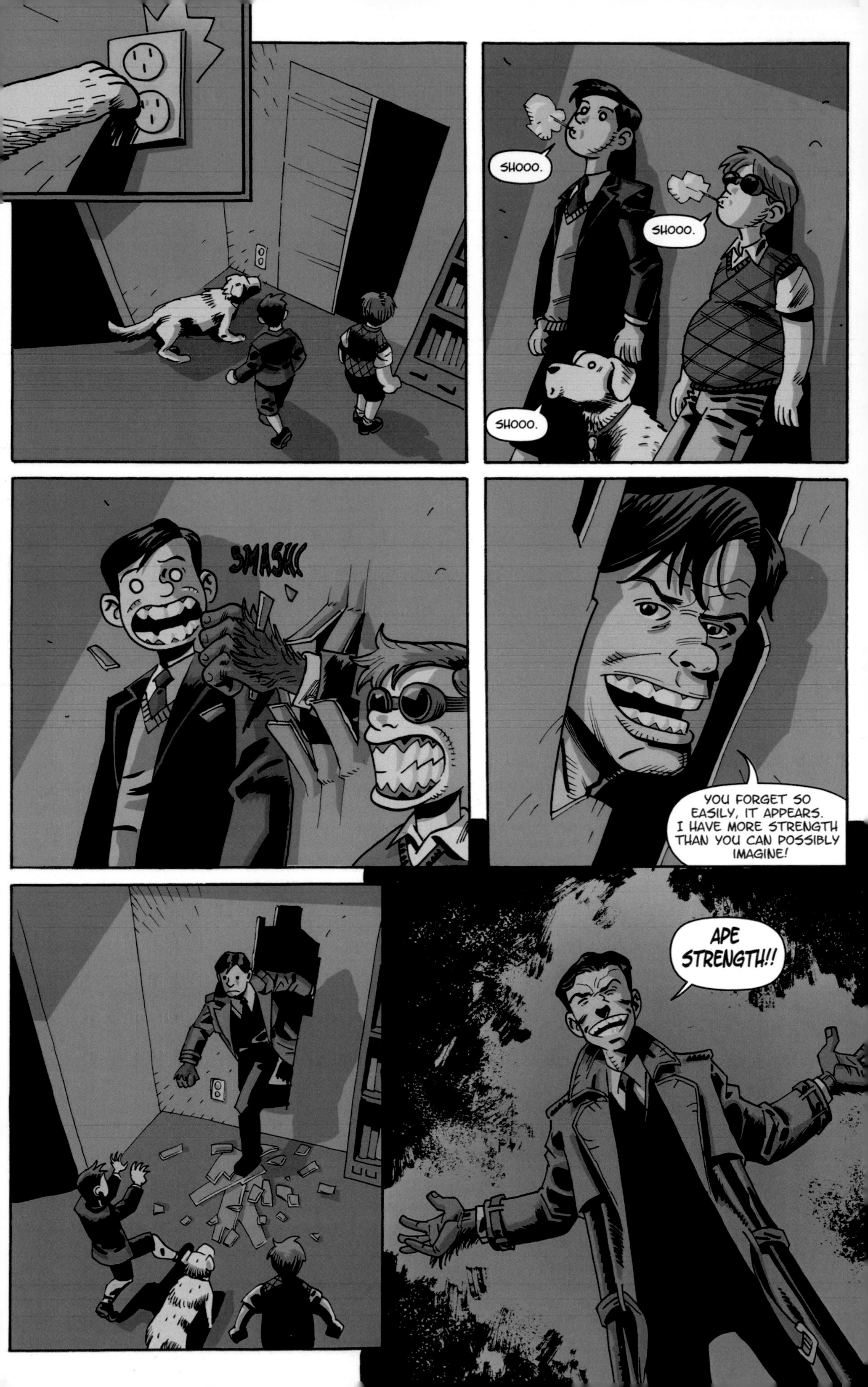
SHOOO.
SHOOO.
SHOOO.
SMASH!
YOU FORGET SO EASILY, IT APPEARS. I HAVE MORE STRENGTH THAN YOU CAN POSSIBLY IMAGINE!
APE STRENGTH!!

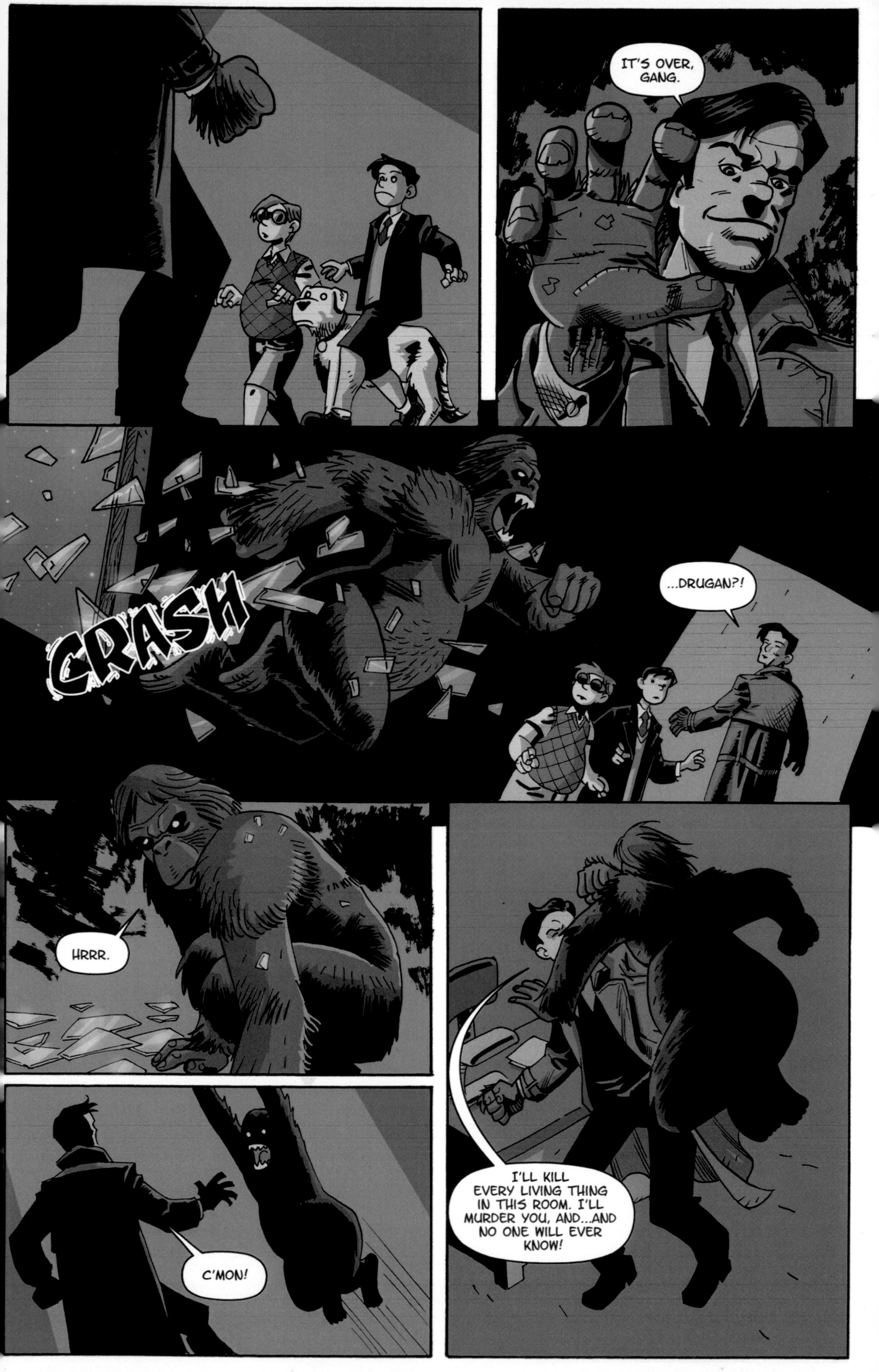
IT'S OVER, GANG.
CRASH
...DRUGAN?!
HRRR.
I'LL KILL EVERY LIVING THING IN THIS ROOM. I'LL MURDER YOU, AND...AND NO ONE WILL EVER KNOW!
C'MON!

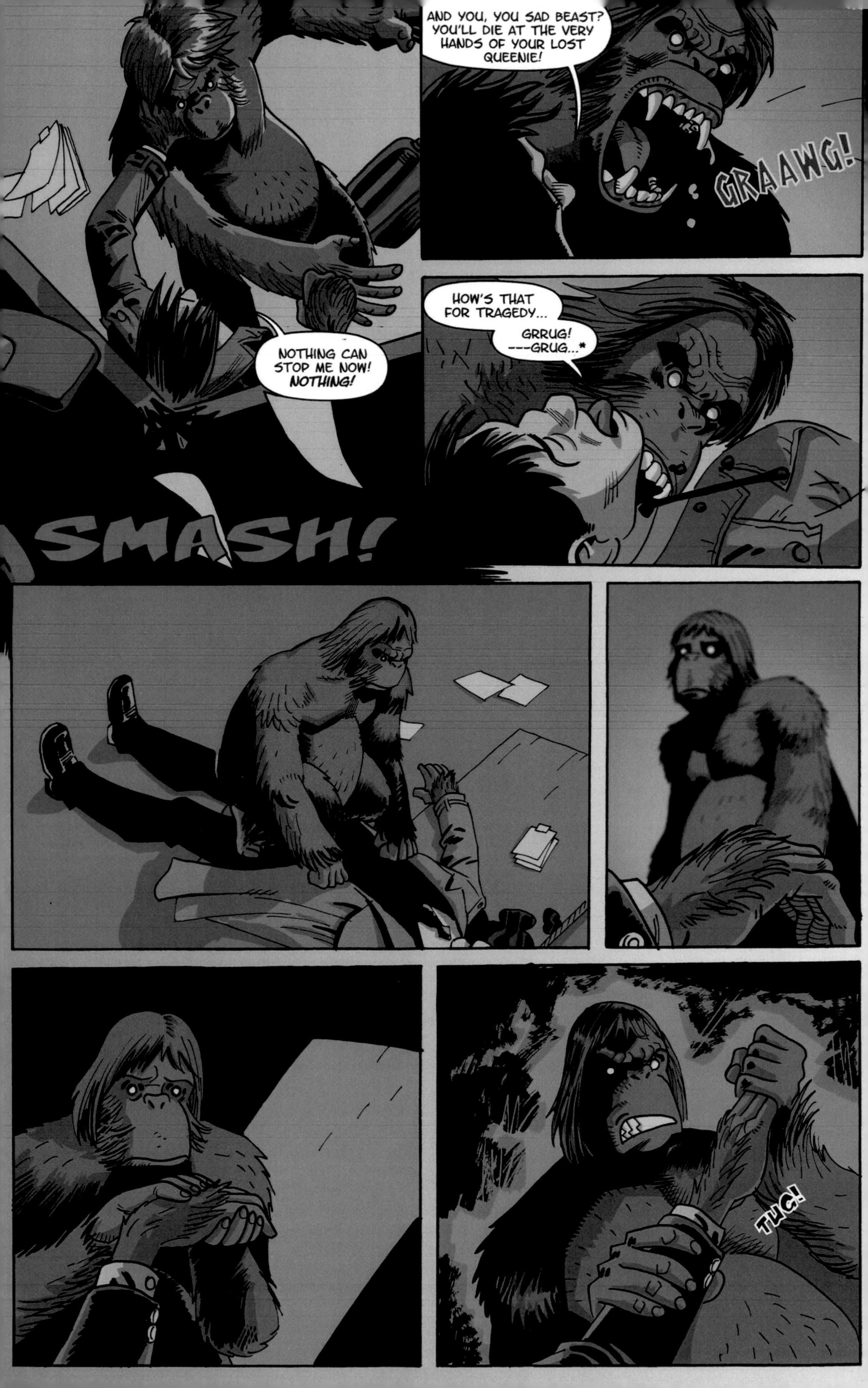
AND YOU, YOU SAD BEAST? YOU'LL DIE AT THE VERY HANDS OF YOUR LOST QUEENIE!
GRAAWG!
NOTHING CAN STOP ME NOW! NOTHING!
HOW'S THAT FOR TRAGEDY...
GRRUG! ---GRUG...*
SMASH!
TUG!

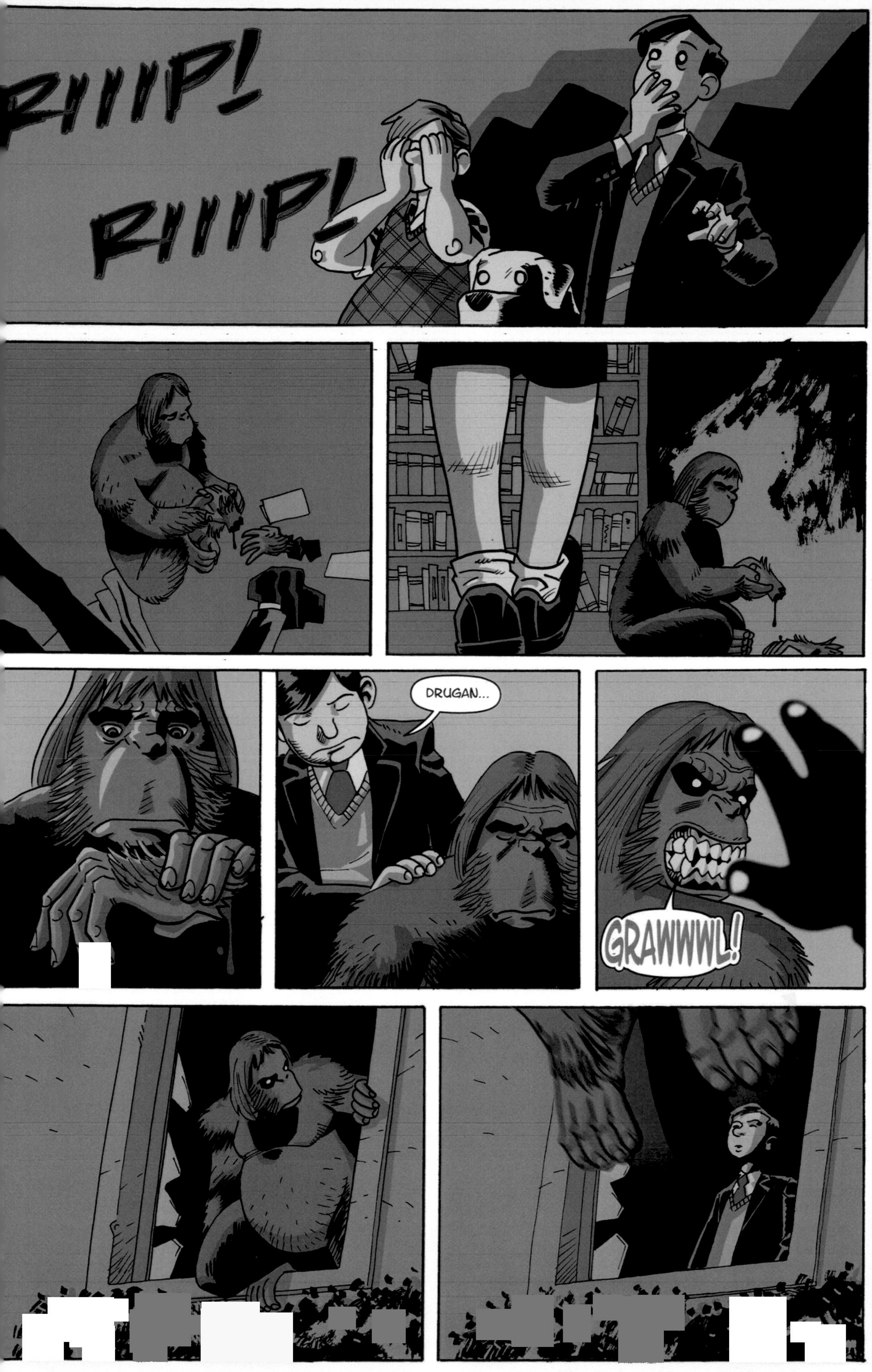
RIIIIP!
RIIIIP!
DRUGAN...
GRAWWWL!

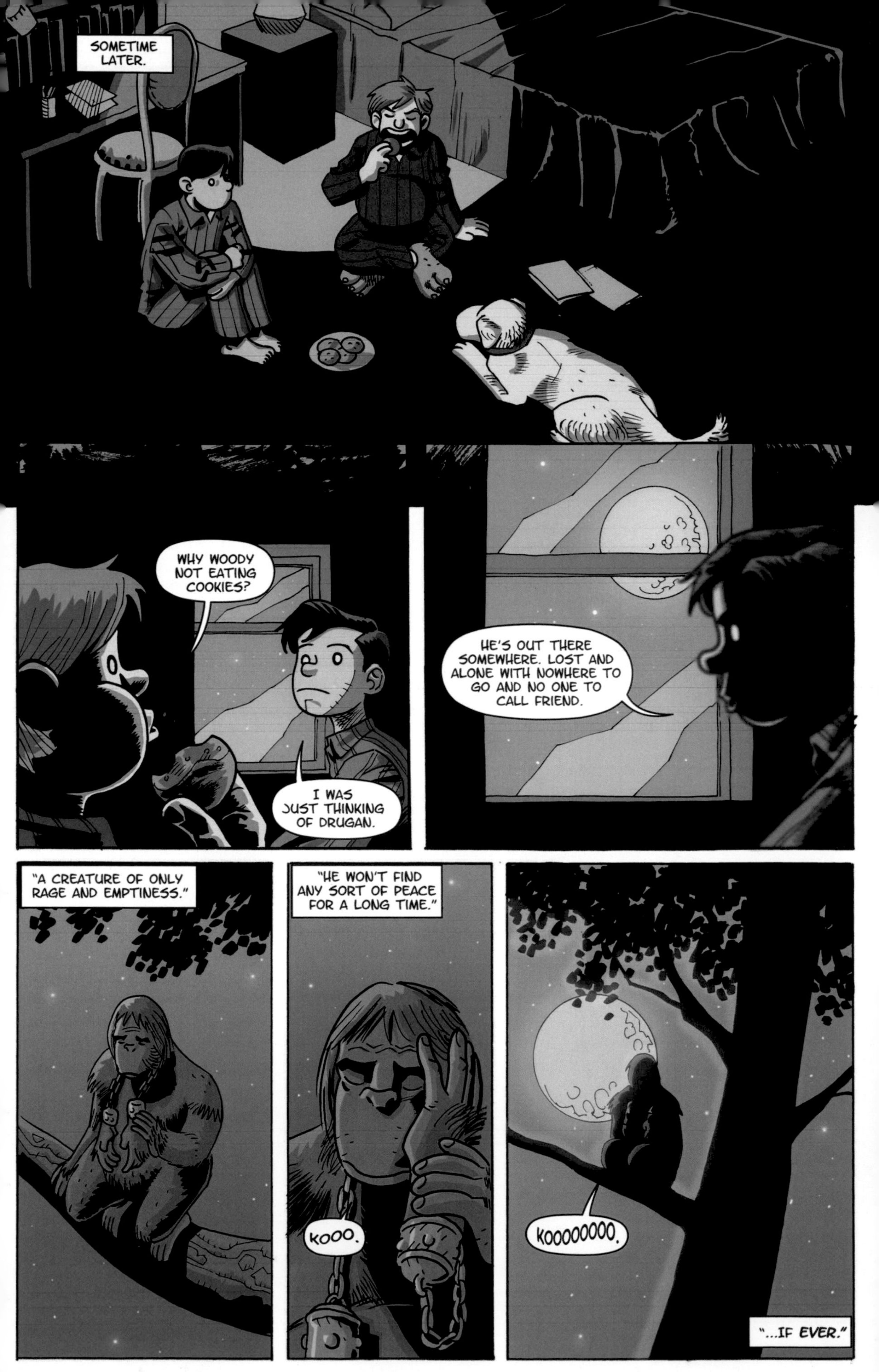
SOMETIME LATER.
WHY WOODY NOT EATING COOKIES?
I WAS JUST THINKING OF DRUGAN.
HE'S OUT THERE SOMEWHERE. LOST AND ALONE WITH NOWHERE TO GO AND NO ONE TO CALL FRIEND.
"A CREATURE OF ONLY RAGE AND EMPTINESS."
"HE WON'T FIND ANY SORT OF PEACE FOR A LONG TIME."
KOOO.
KOOOOOOOO.
"...IF EVER."

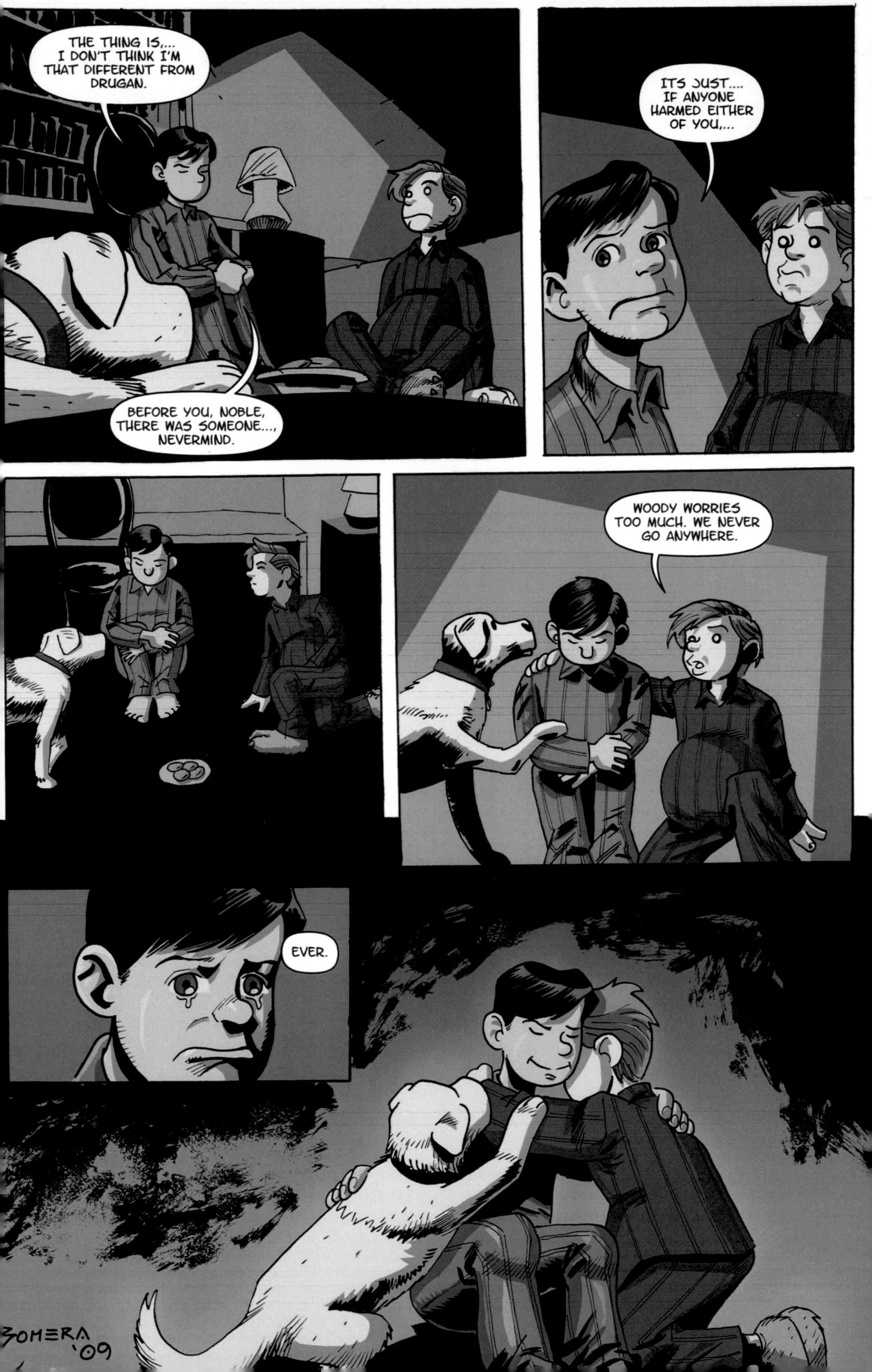
THE THING IS,... I DON'T THINK I'M THAT DIFFERENT FROM DRUGAN.
BEFORE YOU, NOBLE, THERE WAS SOMEONE..., NEVERMIND.
ITS JUST.... IF ANYONE HARMED EITHER OF YOU,...
WOODY WORRIES TOO MUCH. WE NEVER GO ANYWHERE.
EVER.
ZOMERA '09

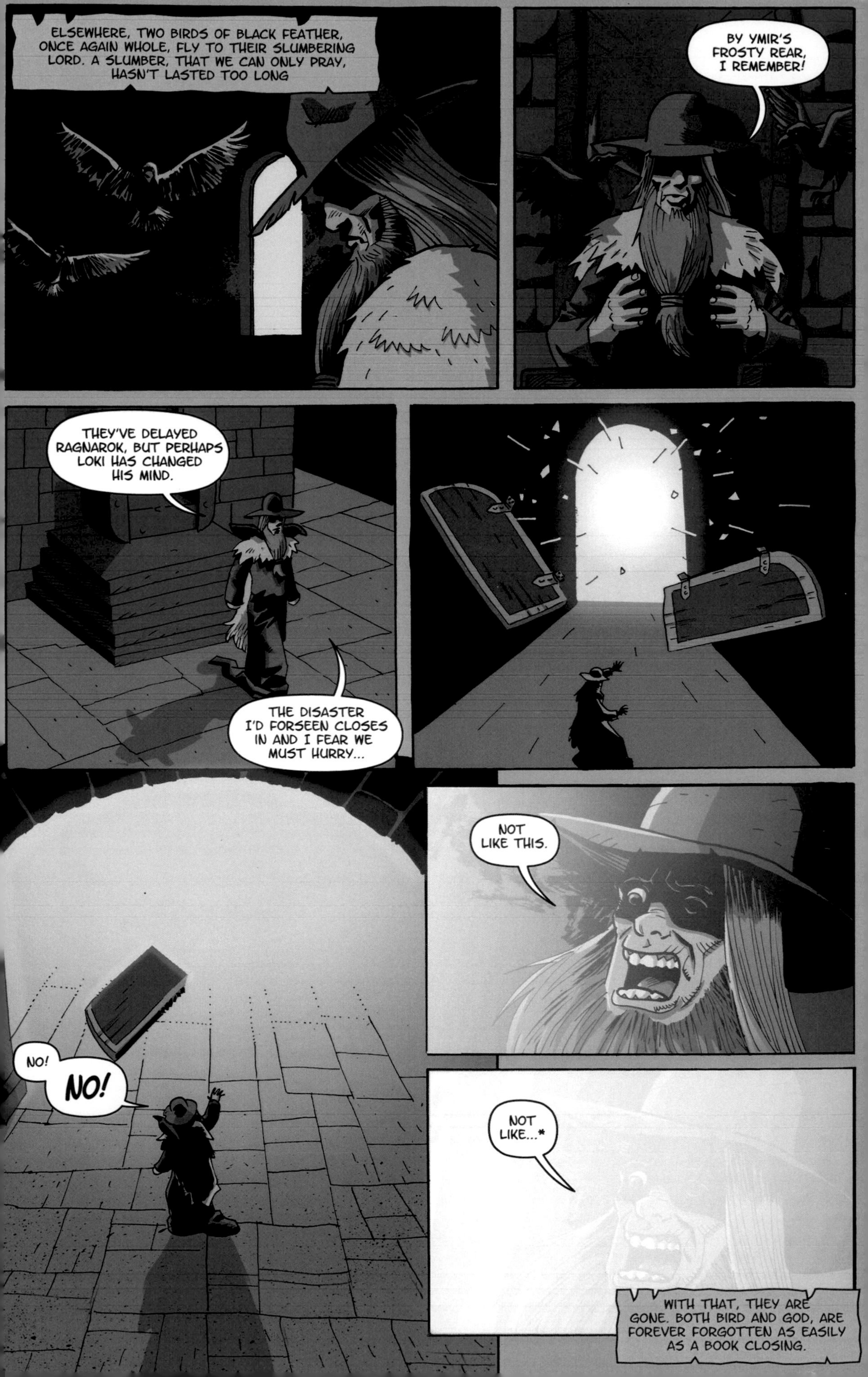
ELSEWHERE, TWO BIRDS OF BLACK FEATHER, ONCE AGAIN WHOLE, FLY TO THEIR SLUMBERING LORD. A SLUMBER, THAT WE CAN ONLY PRAY, HASN'T LASTED TOO LONG
BY YMIR'S FROSTY REAR, I REMEMBER!
THEY'VE DELAYED RAGNAROK, BUT PERHAPS LOKI HAS CHANGED HIS MIND.
THE DISASTER I'D FORSEEN CLOSES IN AND I FEAR WE MUST HURRY...
NO! NO!
NOT LIKE THIS.
NOT LIKE...*
WITH THAT, THEY ARE GONE. BOTH BIRD AND GOD, ARE FOREVER FORGOTTEN AS EASILY AS A BOOK CLOSING.

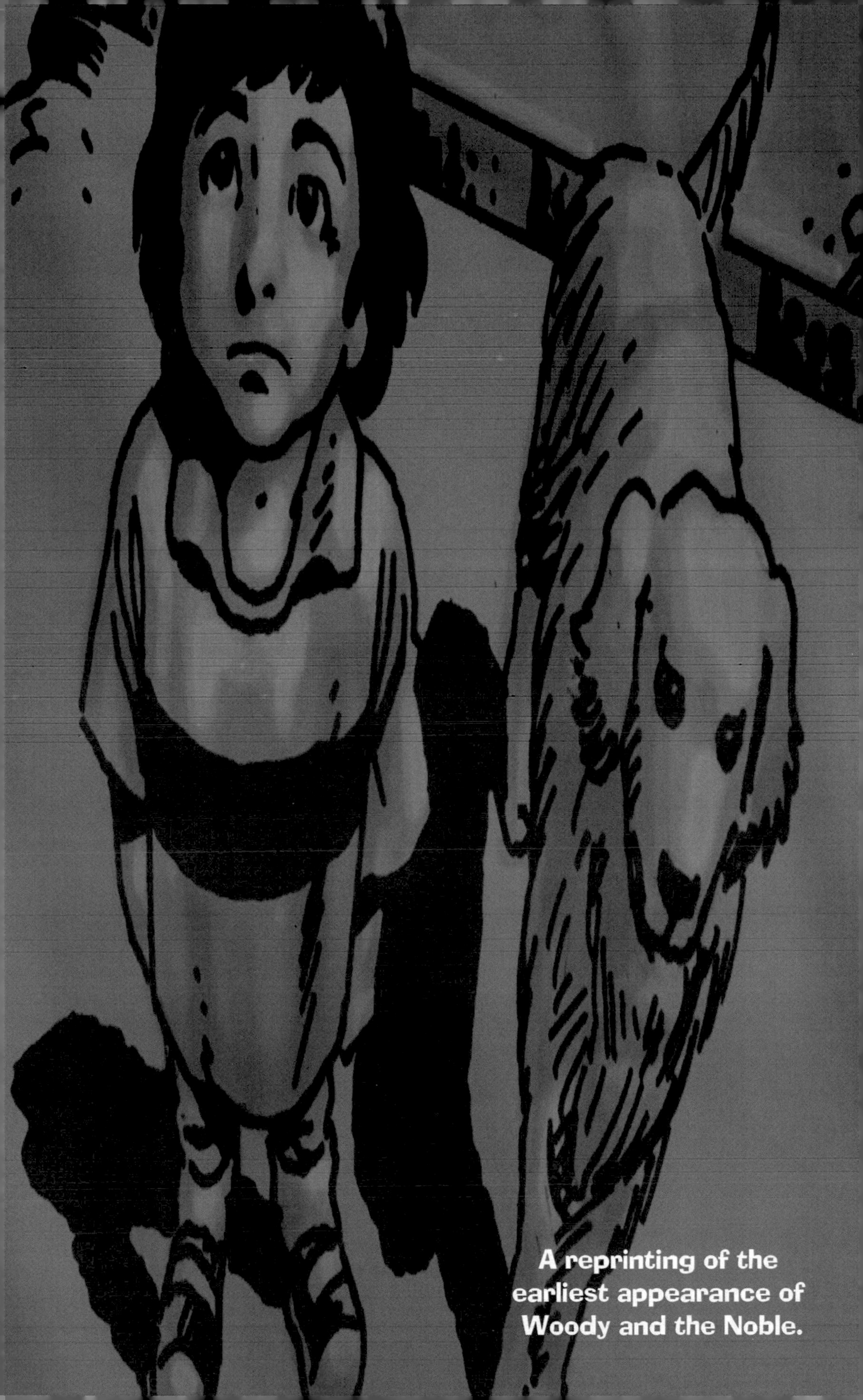

A reprinting of the earliest appearance of Woody and the Noble.

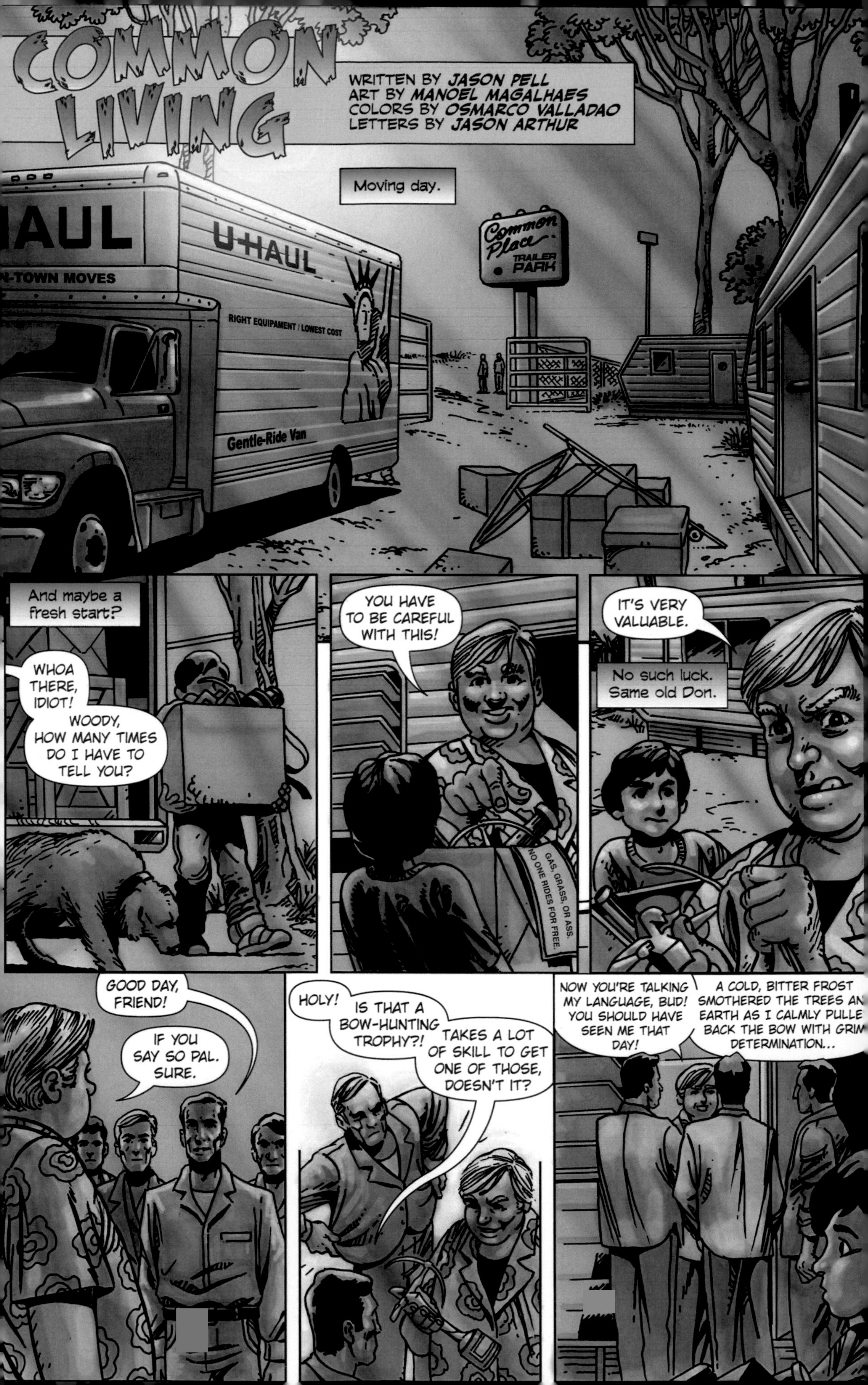
COMMON LIVING
WRITTEN BY JASON PELL
ART BY MANOEL MAGALHAES
COLORS BY OSMARCO VALLADAO
LETTERS BY JASON ARTHUR
Moving day.
U-HAUL
IN-TOWN MOVES
RIGHT EQUIPAMENT / LOWEST COST
Gentle-Ride Van
Common Place TRAILER PARK
And maybe a fresh start?
WHOA THERE, IDIOT!
WOODY, HOW MANY TIMES DO I HAVE TO TELL YOU?
YOU HAVE TO BE CAREFUL WITH THIS!
GAS, GRASS, OR ASS. NO ONE RIDES FOR FREE.
IT'S VERY VALUABLE.
No such luck. Same old Don.
GOOD DAY, FRIEND!
IF YOU SAY SO PAL. SURE.
HOLY!
IS THAT A BOW-HUNTING TROPHY?!
TAKES A LOT OF SKILL TO GET ONE OF THOSE, DOESN'T IT?
NOW YOU'RE TALKING MY LANGUAGE, BUD! YOU SHOULD HAVE SEEN ME THAT DAY!
A COLD, BITTER FROST SMOTHERED THE TREES AN EARTH AS I CALMLY PULLE BACK THE BOW WITH GRIM DETERMINATION...

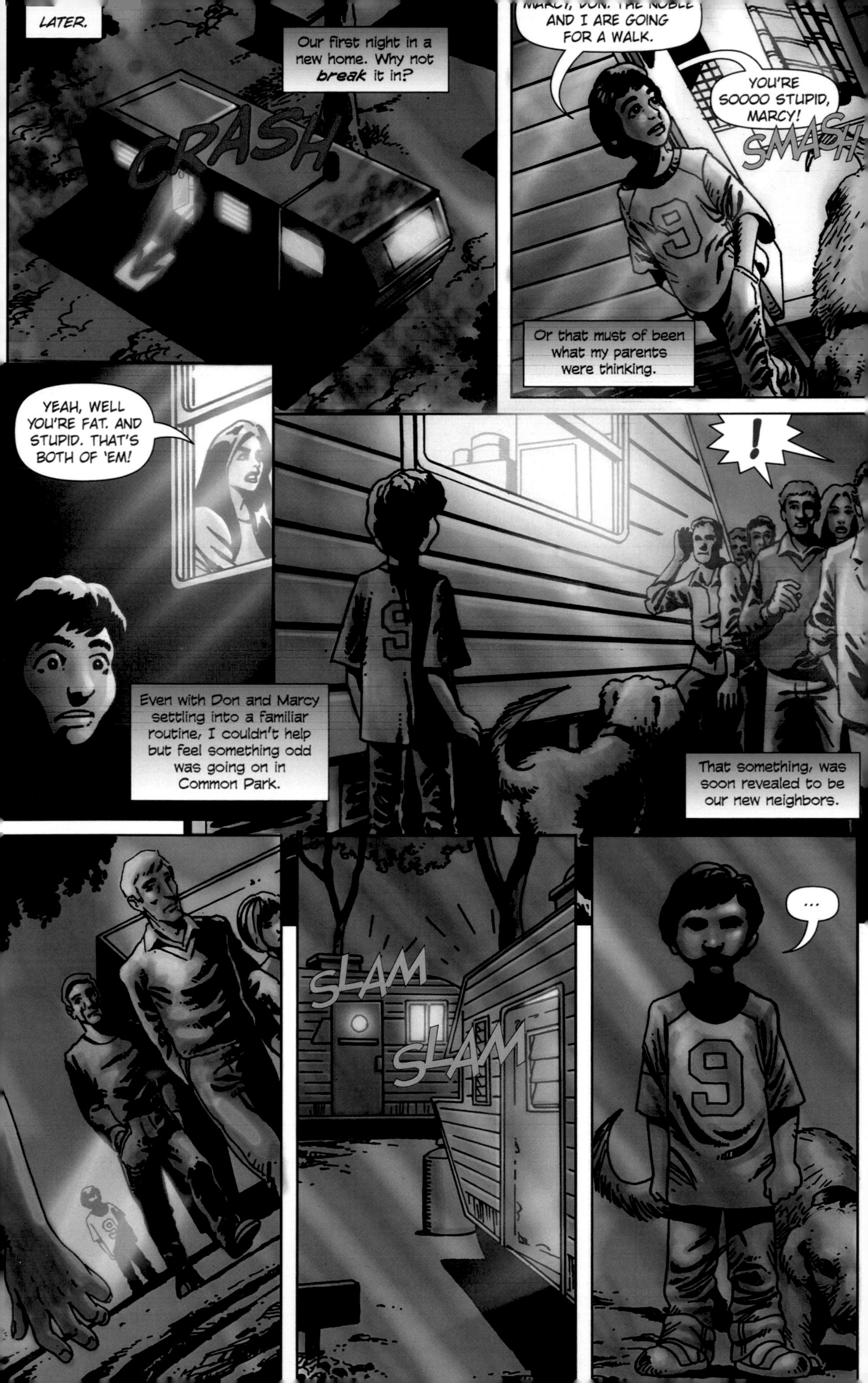
LATER.
Our first night in a new home. Why not **break** it in?
CRASH
MARCY, DON. THE NOBLE AND I ARE GOING FOR A WALK.
YOU'RE SOOOO STUPID, MARCY!
SMASH
Or that must of been what my parents were thinking.
YEAH, WELL YOU'RE FAT. AND STUPID. THAT'S BOTH OF 'EM!
Even with Don and Marcy settling into a familiar routine, I couldn't help but feel something odd was going on in Common Park.
!
That something, was soon revealed to be our new neighbors.
SLAM
SLAM
...

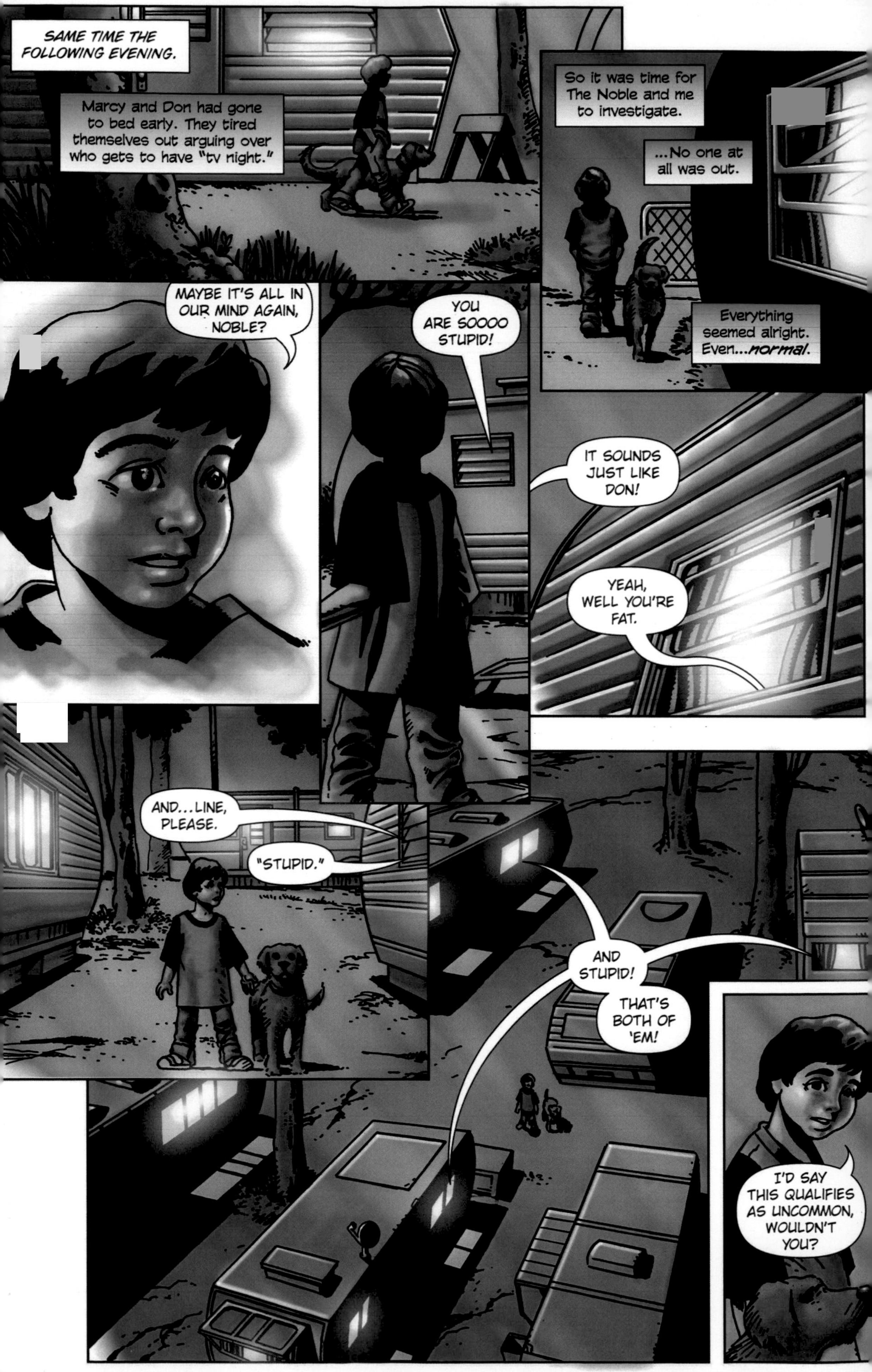
SAME TIME THE FOLLOWING EVENING.
Marcy and Don had gone to bed early. They tired themselves out arguing over who gets to have "tv night."
So it was time for The Noble and me to investigate.
...No one at all was out.
Everything seemed alright. Even...*normal*.
MAYBE IT'S ALL IN OUR MIND AGAIN, NOBLE?
YOU ARE SOOOO STUPID!
IT SOUNDS JUST LIKE DON!
YEAH, WELL YOU'RE FAT.
AND...LINE, PLEASE.
"STUPID."
AND STUPID!
THAT'S BOTH OF 'EM!
I'D SAY THIS QUALIFIES AS UNCOMMON, WOULDN'T YOU?

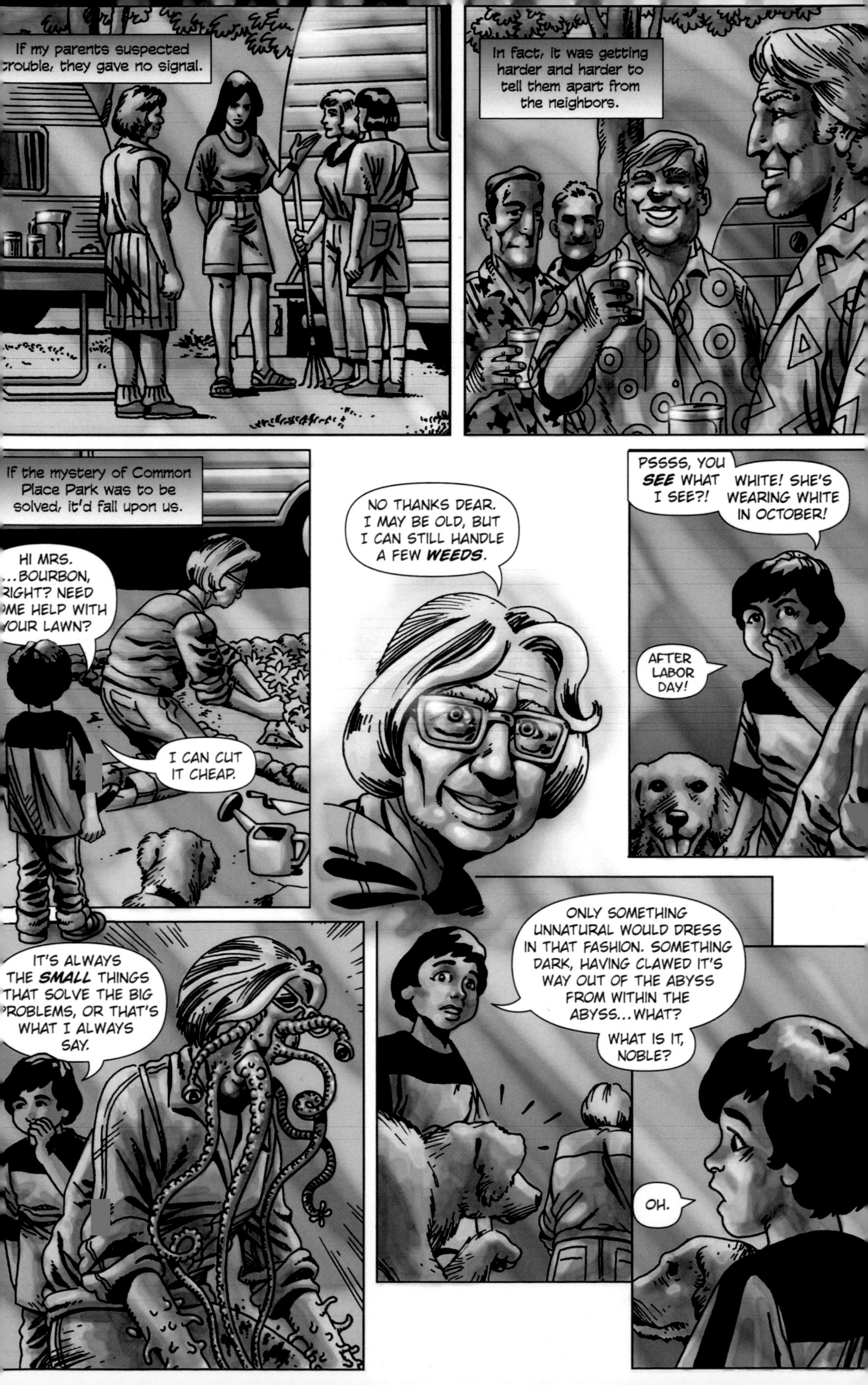

If my parents suspected trouble, they gave no signal.
In fact, it was getting harder and harder to tell them apart from the neighbors.
If the mystery of Common Place Park was to be solved, it'd fall upon us.
HI MRS. ...BOURBON, RIGHT? NEED SOME HELP WITH YOUR LAWN?
I CAN CUT IT CHEAP.
NO THANKS DEAR. I MAY BE OLD, BUT I CAN STILL HANDLE A FEW WEEDS.
PSSSS, YOU SEE WHAT I SEE?!
WHITE! SHE'S WEARING WHITE IN OCTOBER!
AFTER LABOR DAY!
IT'S ALWAYS THE SMALL THINGS THAT SOLVE THE BIG PROBLEMS, OR THAT'S WHAT I ALWAYS SAY.
ONLY SOMETHING UNNATURAL WOULD DRESS IN THAT FASHION. SOMETHING DARK, HAVING CLAWED IT'S WAY OUT OF THE ABYSS FROM WITHIN THE ABYSS...WHAT?
WHAT IS IT, NOBLE?
OH.

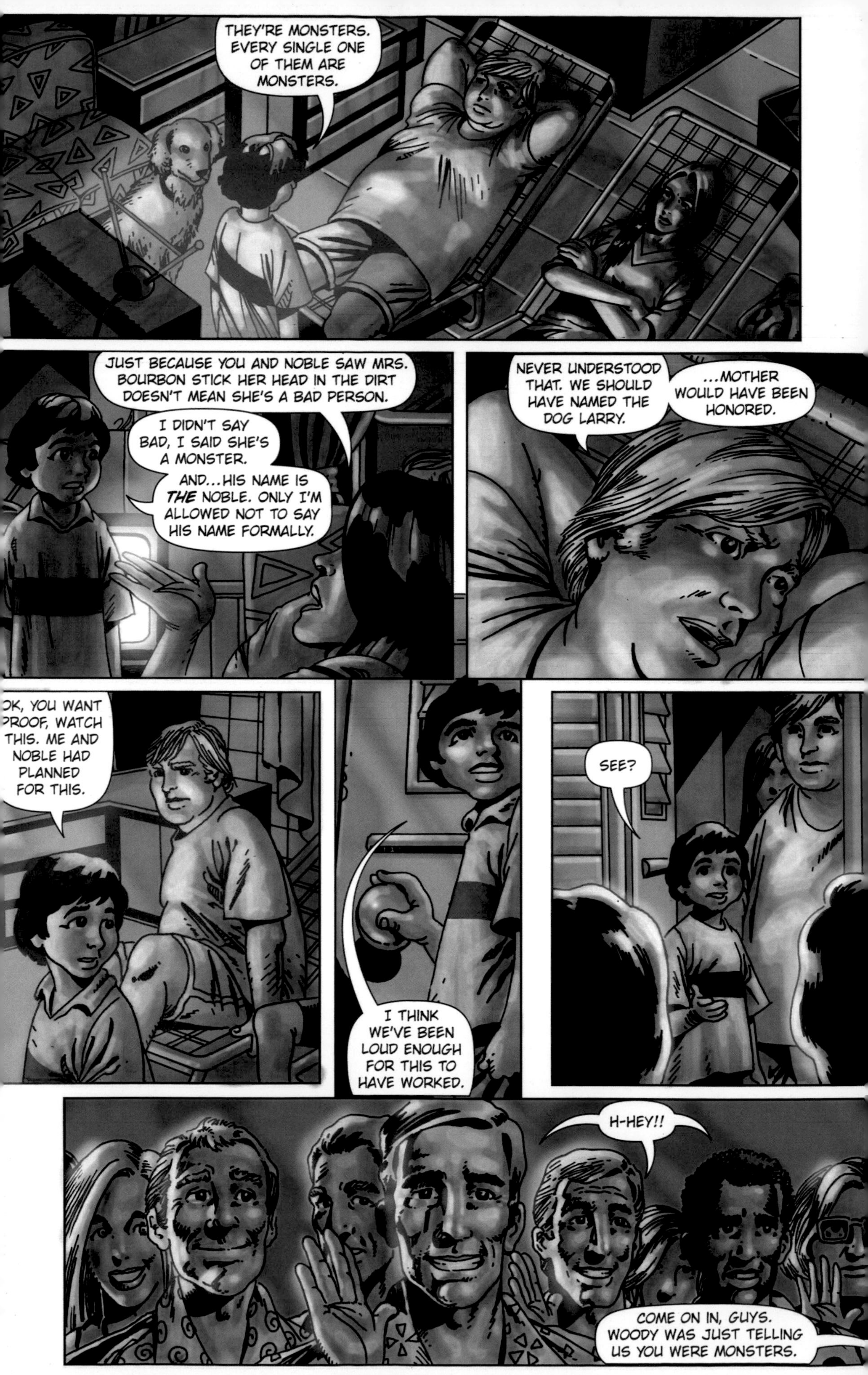
THEY'RE MONSTERS. EVERY SINGLE ONE OF THEM ARE MONSTERS.
JUST BECAUSE YOU AND NOBLE SAW MRS. BOURBON STICK HER HEAD IN THE DIRT DOESN'T MEAN SHE'S A BAD PERSON.
I DIDN'T SAY BAD, I SAID SHE'S A MONSTER.
AND...HIS NAME IS THE NOBLE. ONLY I'M ALLOWED NOT TO SAY HIS NAME FORMALLY.
NEVER UNDERSTOOD THAT. WE SHOULD HAVE NAMED THE DOG LARRY.
...MOTHER WOULD HAVE BEEN HONORED.
OK, YOU WANT PROOF, WATCH THIS. ME AND NOBLE HAD PLANNED FOR THIS.
I THINK WE'VE BEEN LOUD ENOUGH FOR THIS TO HAVE WORKED.
SEE?
H-HEY!!
COME ON IN, GUYS. WOODY WAS JUST TELLING US YOU WERE MONSTERS.

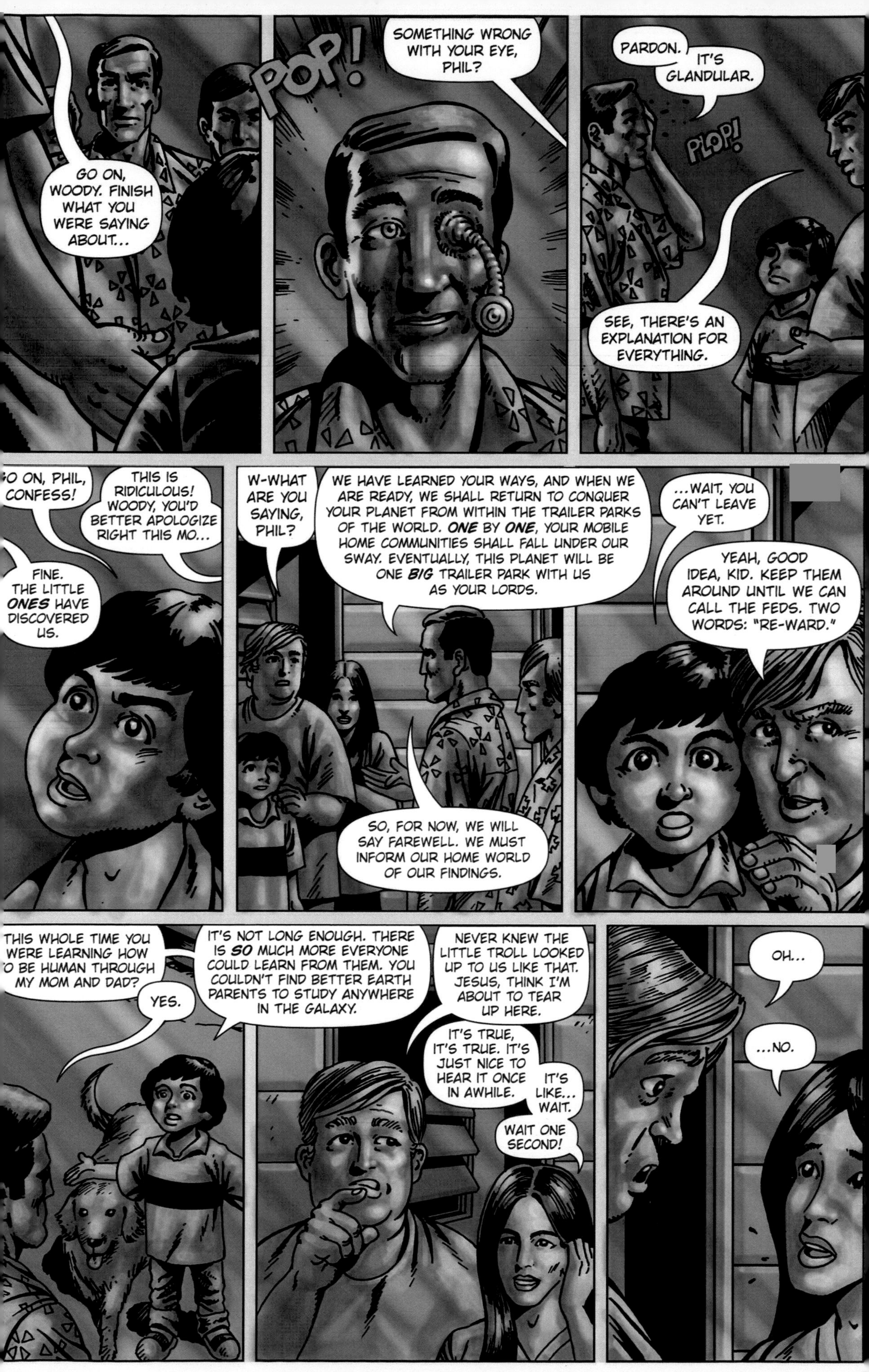
GO ON, WOODY. FINISH WHAT YOU WERE SAYING ABOUT...
POP!
SOMETHING WRONG WITH YOUR EYE, PHIL?
PARDON.
IT'S GLANDULAR.
PLOP!
SEE, THERE'S AN EXPLANATION FOR EVERYTHING.
GO ON, PHIL, CONFESS!
THIS IS RIDICULOUS! WOODY, YOU'D BETTER APOLOGIZE RIGHT THIS MO...
FINE. THE LITTLE ONES HAVE DISCOVERED US.
W-WHAT ARE YOU SAYING, PHIL?
WE HAVE LEARNED YOUR WAYS, AND WHEN WE ARE READY, WE SHALL RETURN TO CONQUER YOUR PLANET FROM WITHIN THE TRAILER PARKS OF THE WORLD. ONE BY ONE, YOUR MOBILE HOME COMMUNITIES SHALL FALL UNDER OUR SWAY. EVENTUALLY, THIS PLANET WILL BE ONE BIG TRAILER PARK WITH US AS YOUR LORDS.
SO, FOR NOW, WE WILL SAY FAREWELL. WE MUST INFORM OUR HOME WORLD OF OUR FINDINGS.
...WAIT, YOU CAN'T LEAVE YET.
YEAH, GOOD IDEA, KID. KEEP THEM AROUND UNTIL WE CAN CALL THE FEDS. TWO WORDS: "RE-WARD."
THIS WHOLE TIME YOU WERE LEARNING HOW TO BE HUMAN THROUGH MY MOM AND DAD?
YES.
IT'S NOT LONG ENOUGH. THERE IS SO MUCH MORE EVERYONE COULD LEARN FROM THEM. YOU COULDN'T FIND BETTER EARTH PARENTS TO STUDY ANYWHERE IN THE GALAXY.
NEVER KNEW THE LITTLE TROLL LOOKED UP TO US LIKE THAT. JESUS, THINK I'M ABOUT TO TEAR UP HERE.
IT'S TRUE, IT'S TRUE. IT'S JUST NICE TO HEAR IT ONCE IN AWHILE.
IT'S LIKE... WAIT.
WAIT ONE SECOND!
OH...
...NO.

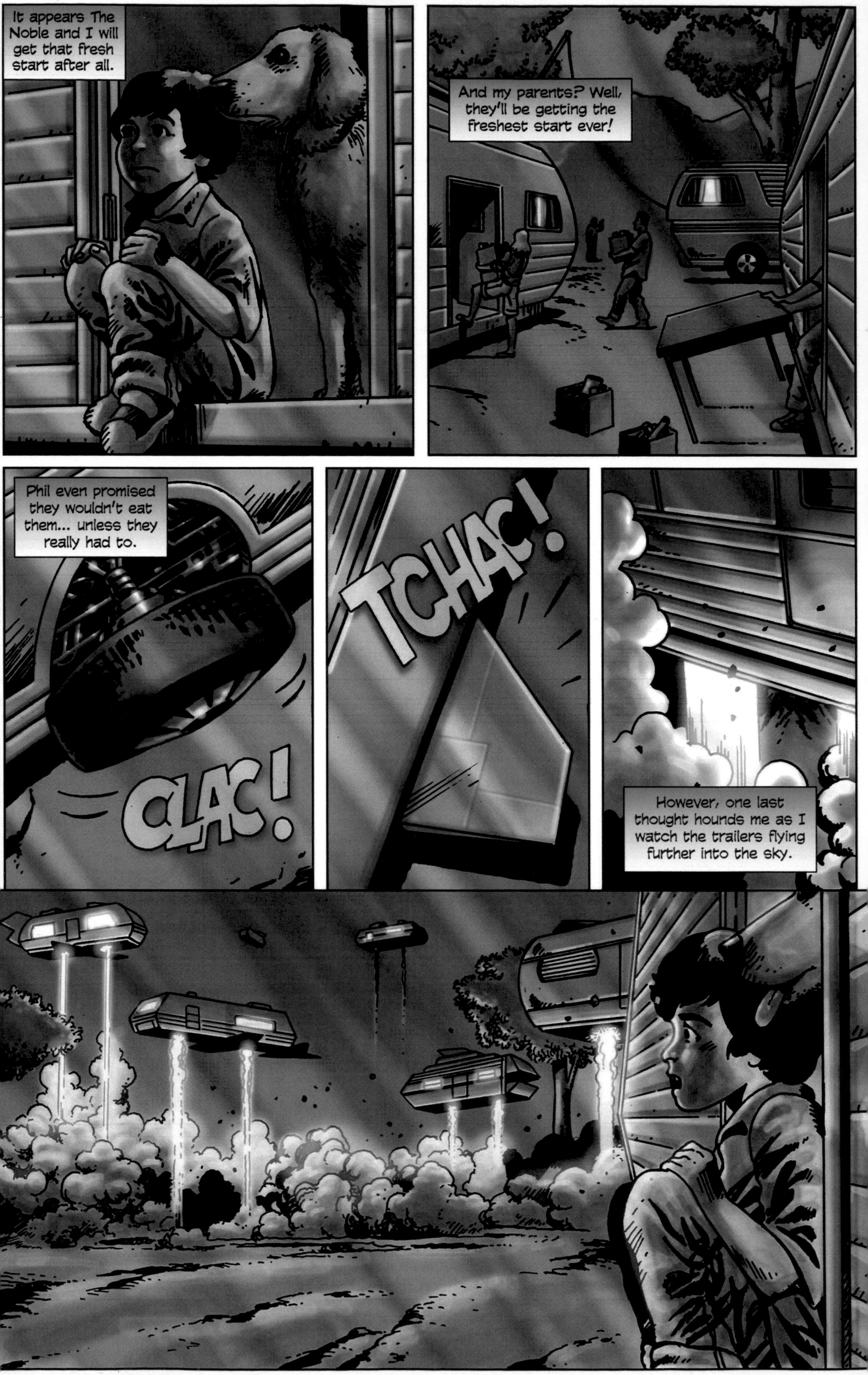
It appears The Noble and I will get that fresh start after all.
And my parents? Well, they'll be getting the freshest start ever!
Phil even promised they wouldn't eat them... unless they really had to.
CLAC!
TCHAC!
However, one last thought hounds me as I watch the trailers flying further into the sky.

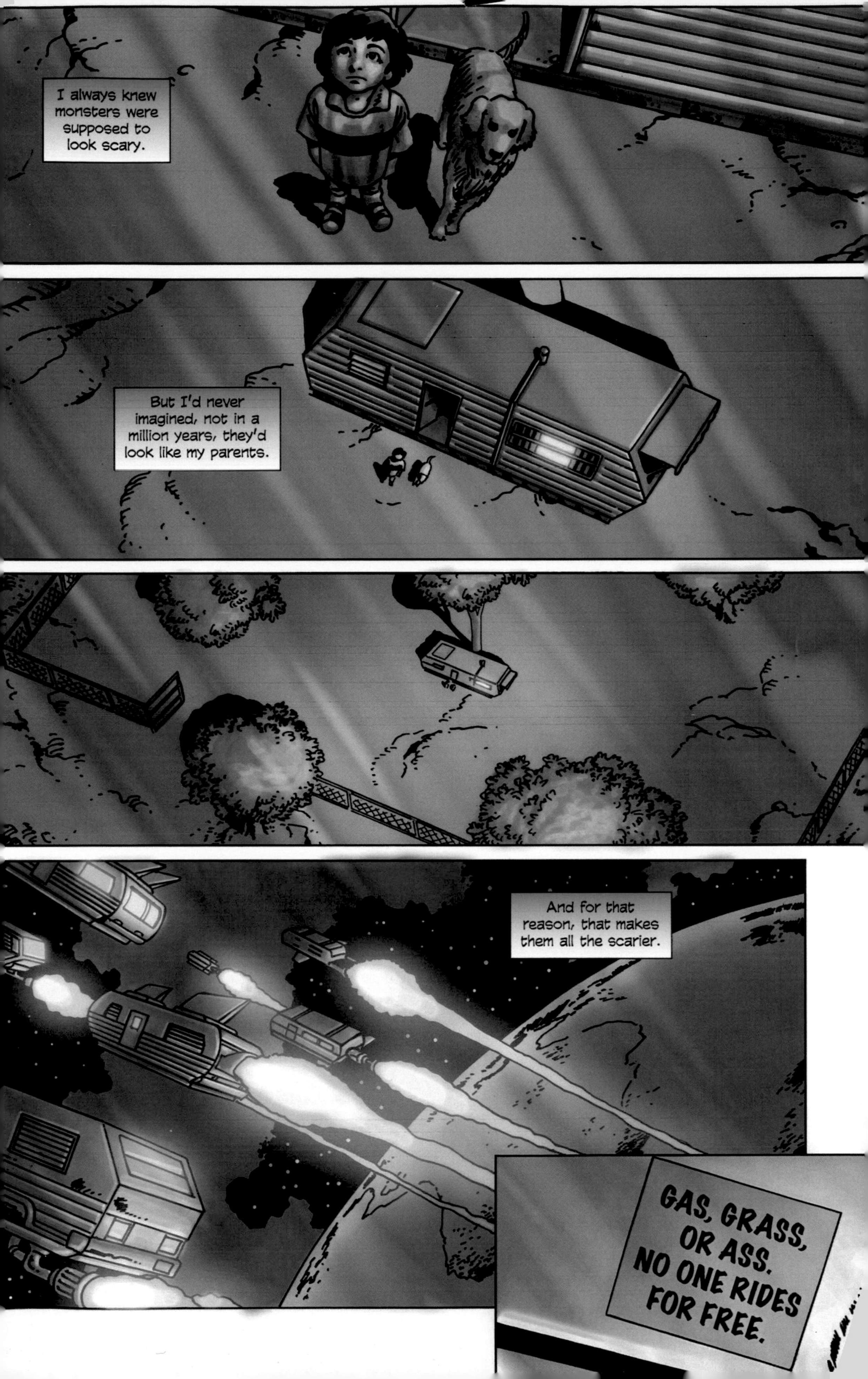
I always knew monsters were supposed to look scary.
But I'd never imagined, not in a million years, they'd look like my parents.
And for that reason, that makes them all the scarier.
GAS, GRASS, OR ASS. NO ONE RIDES FOR FREE.

In remembrance of Odin